Voice of the Trees

COMPANION

MICKIE MUELLER

Llewellyn Publications
WOODBURY, MINNESOTA

FIRST EDITION
Second Printing, 2014

Book design by Rebecca Zins
Cover and interior artwork © 2011 Mickie Mueller
Cover design by Adrienne W. Zimiga
Leaf endpages © iStockphoto/Sergey Titov

Llewellyn Publications is a registered trademark of Llewellyn Worldwide Ltd.
ISBN 978-0-7387-1554-4

The *Voice of the Trees* kit consists of a boxed set of
25 full-color cards and this perfect-bound book.

Llewellyn Publications
A Division of Llewellyn Worldwide Ltd.
2143 Wooddale Drive
Woodbury, MN 55125-2989
www.llewellyn.com
Printed in the United States of America

Voice of the Trees
COMPANION

About the Author and Artist

ickie Mueller is an award-winning artist of fantasy, fairy, and myth. She has been working as a freelance artist since 1983. She is a longtime contributor to her local alternative faith community and has studied natural magic, Celtic tradition, and the Old Ways tradition. In addition, she has been a Reiki healing master/teacher in the Usui Shiki Royoho tradition since 2001. She is a member of the MAFIA (Missouri Area Fantasy Illustrators Association) and is the illustrator of the critically acclaimed divination decks *The Well Worn Path* and *The Hidden Path*. A regular article and illustration contributor to *Llewellyn's Magical Almanac*, Mickie has also published both articles and artwork in *Witchcraft & Wicca Magazine* in the UK as well as *The Witches' Voice*, *Magickal Light Magazine*, and several other online publications.

Mickie's art has been seen internationally on the covers of *Witchcraft & Wicca*, *Raven's Call*, *Spirit Seeker*, and *Oracle 2000*, to name a few. Mickie creates her art magically, lovingly using infusions of herbs corresponding with the subject matter she portrays. She works by hand in a mixed media of watercolor and colored pencil. Her magical artwork can be seen on her website at www.mickiemuellerart.com.

Contents

Acknowledgments

There are so many people who supported me along the way, and while I can't list them all here, there are many who actually became a part of this project; without them, it would not be what it has become.

First and foremost, my husband Dan, my best friend, manager, research genius, occasional model, and overall partner in crime. Without his support, none of what I do would ever be possible. My great kids, Brittany, Chelsea, and Tristan, for always being excited about my work, even when it kept me busy—but never too busy for their sweet faces.

Thanks to Rev. Ron Berry for loaning me a stack of books from his old OBOD days.

All of these good folks I've mentioned so far were also happy to "come here and stand like this," modeling for reference photos for these cards, as were some other kind, brave, and patient people. P. J., Andrew, Darleen, Ken, Ember, Mark, Sarah, Draco, Ellen, Hailey, Taylor, and Lisa, my oldest friend, all posed as the people of the Celtic clans within this deck. Thanks to Andrew and Pete for photographing a couple of them for me and staying true to my vision. To Mom, Dad, and Robin for teaching me the real meaning of a clan, a family. To the ladies of Greenwood for field-testing the tree devotionals.

To Barbara Moore, my acquisitions editor, for being there from the beginning to nurture this grove, and to Becky Zins, for her wonderful eye and magical editing powers and for saying, "Yes, do more illustrations for the book!" To Lisa Hunt for her kindness, wisdom, and for being my hero when I really needed one. To the Spirit of Olde for helping me procure some of my harder-to-get samples of Celtic tree wood gathered from mystical areas in Britain. To Treesforlife.org.uk for facilitating the living Voice of the Trees grove in the Scottish Highlands.

Last but not least, thank you to the trees, for sharing their stories with me and for trusting me to share them with you.

Preface

As a young girl, I remember gazing out my window on a quiet winter day at the branches of the poplar tree that grew in my front yard. I traced the lines of each branch that stood out against the cold, gray sky and knew there were answers to some deep mystery that lay in its patterns. It made me ponder why the tree grew as it did and how it rested now, quietly, in its wintry sleep. I imagined the tree's roots deep beneath the ground, and I knew that they mirrored the branches that stretched upward. I also knew that the patterns were similar to the patterns of my own vascular and nervous systems. We had been studying these systems in school, and at the time I had noticed the similarity and recalled it while looking at the branches. I wondered what else we had in common with trees; are we somehow part of each other, or perhaps part of something grander than all of humankind and all the forests of trees? These were the kinds of thoughts that often kept me from finishing my math homework. But science was fascinating and often brought up more questions than it answered. Having been an artist all my life, I was always quick to notice patterns and similarities—how things fit together in a big, beautiful tapestry. I knew the tree drew nutrients from below the earth as well as from the sun above through its leaves in the summer. At the time, I had never heard of the phrase "As above, so below," but I was learning the beginnings of this concept, and of oneness as well, as I studied the branches and contemplated what lessons this tree had for me.

For ages, trees have been revered for many reasons by humankind. We use trees for shelter, we harvest food from them, and we have made weapons and shields from their wood to protect ourselves and to hunt game. Trees have provided wood for the fires that kept us warm and cooked our food, and we have shared fellowship, stories, and ritual around fires fed by the trees of the earth. One of the most valuable inventions of the modern age—books, the bringers of knowledge—would not be available to us if not for trees. The book you hold in your hands and the cards that will soon take you on a journey of tree wisdom and divination both came from trees. We treasure these things that came from trees, and we keep them safe. Large corporations have finally realized the importance of trees as they all scramble to become more "green" and focus on sustainability, joining organizations like the Forestry Initiative in an effort to undo the damage the environment has suffered. The trees of this planet are often used as symbolic reminders of our stewardship of this planet. Trees have touched our lives on so many levels that they have become a part of us forever.

The tree has long been a sacred symbol revered by shamans, druids, witches, and mystics throughout the ages. The sacred tree represents the three mystical realms. Its branches that reach up into the sky and give home to many birds considered messengers of the gods are a gateway to the upper spiritual realm. This realm is how we access our higher powers and connect with deity and universal power. Its trunk, which is the part of the tree most easily accessible to humankind, represents the physical world, or middle realm. A knothole in a tree trunk can be used as a passageway for the shaman to spiritually travel through time and space in the physical realm, as well as find access to other realms. The middle realm is the place where we connect to the concept of oneness, reminding us that we are all connected to everyone and everything. The roots deep beneath the earth are the gateway to the lower spiritual realms where we can find the deep inner mysteries of birth and rebirth, our shadow selves, the strength of our ancestors, and the power of the earth. These ancient lessons of the trees cross many cultures.

Most of us connect with trees on a much more basic level than that of the shamanic journey. When we are near trees, they make us feel peaceful. The light filtering through their green leaves on a summer afternoon can soothe our spirits, fill our hearts with joy, and make us feel young and free. We plant altars of flowers around them in our gardens and hang bird feeders from their branches so we can make offerings to nature. Driving past a wooded area, we might imagine an escape from our worries, getting lost in the trees, and for that moment—when our thoughts turn to images of running through the woods—we revisit a much older time when trees made our ancestors feel safe. When we plant a tree, we feel a great feeling of accomplishment, because we know that it will become something greater as it grows and that our action has helped our environment. Trees are still our shelter, our connection with sacred nature, and a healing force in our lives every day.

A Note on the Art

My purpose in designing this deck was to share the Celtic tree ogham with modern practitioners of various earth spirituality paths and cartomancers, as well as those who wish to more deeply explore their Celtic heritage. The ogham is an ancient and intriguing system of letters and divination dated as far back as the fourth century. I wanted to make this system more readily available to those who wish to learn its magical teachings. There are several references in legends of the ogham having been used in divination by carving the fews, or letters/ symbols, upon sticks of wood. The tree ogham has been used in modern times as an oracle by carving each few on a stick (called a stave) or on a wooden tile, casting them, and reading the meanings, much in the same way that runes are used. I portrayed each symbol, or few, on the corresponding card, as well as a pictorial representation of both the tree and the meaning, to further assist the modern reader in a more intuitive reading using this ancient system.

The illustrations in this oracle are intended to be used as a visual tutorial to the enigmatic ogham system. Here, I show more than just the tree alone—I wanted to go further, to portray the *meaning behind* each tree. Each image has the tree on the card incorporated with some kind of action involving either the people or animals of the Celtic lands. In doing this, I wanted to show that our interaction with the trees is important, and also to make each card more intuitive so that when you look at each one, the image triggers an emotional response, telling you the story of what the card means.

It has been said that in order to get the greatest connection with each tree, it is best to use all the woods—the original twenty and the last five, called the forfedha, that were added later—in making your own ogham staves. If you don't live in areas where all of these woods grow, this can turn into quite a costly and challenging task. Therefore, in creating the artwork for each of these cards, I have used a bit of a botanical sample from the corresponding tree (bark, wood, leaf, blossom, etc.) in a magical infusion that was then mixed with my watercolor paints. In this method, the energy of the tree is part of each piece of artwork as well as part of the intuitive process of bringing each card to life. I created this magical tree art with the intention that the energies by which they were created would become a part of every deck of their printed counterparts, including the deck that you now own.

Interestingly, as I worked through each piece of art, I actually went through subtle life experiences associated with each tree's teachings. For instance, while working on the aspen card, which is all about courage and facing your fears, my twenty-year-old daughter ended up in the hospital for a week and was diagnosed with Crohn's disease. She and I faced some serious fears side by side, but we used the strength of our roots to get us through—one of the teachings of the aspen. The week I spent creating the art for the willow card, I had several prophetic dreams and once just got a bad feeling that sent me on the service road instead of my usual route on the highway. I later learned there had been a bad accident on the highway around the time I would have been there. Thankfully, my intuition was working overtime around all the willow energy I was working with. Needless to say, once I noticed this pattern, I made sure to plan the art for cards with potentially darker messages—like yew and blackthorn—for weekends, and I stayed home with my head down and finished them as quickly as possible.

There were also many instances in which I had to use my artistic intuition to make decisions on how each meaning should be portrayed on the card. I went forth with an image, trusting that the spirit of the tree would guide me in the right direction. Oftentimes, after the image had been completed, I would discover a piece of research that would validate my artistic direction and inspiration. Every time that happened, I took this as a sign that this deck wanted to exist and that the lessons of the ogham were waiting to be shared in this way with you. It is my dearest hope that you will gain as much insight using this oracle system as I did in creating it for you.

Introduction
The Celtic Tree Connection

There is some deep tree wisdom that applies to all species of trees in general, such as changing with the seasons, growth, and quiet strength. There are also important teachings that each variety of tree has for us. Each species of tree has specific connections with the world of humans. As magical herbs have different vibrations, correspondences, and uses, so it is true of trees of all geographical locations and cultures. Many people today are familiar with the Celtic tree calendar, a concept that Robert Graves put forth in his 1948 book exploring myth and poetry, *The*

White Goddess. The tree calendar was based upon Graves's study of the ogham. The tree calendar includes only thirteen trees associated with the ogham, naming each of the thirteen moons of the year after a tree. For those familiar with this calendar but who have not studied the ogham, you have just scratched the surface, for there is much more that Celtic tree lore has to teach you. You are about to enter a world of myth and legend that lives through the ages within the spirits of the trees.

The ancient people of the Celtic regions of Europe developed connections with the trees that flourished in those areas. They learned the specific spiritual vibrations, everyday uses, and other properties of those trees, developing lore and legend associated with each species of tree. The assemblage of this knowledge—and its associated symbols and letters—has traversed the years and is preserved for us in the teachings of the tree ogham. Pronunciations of this system are as wide and varied as the different dialects of the Celtic regions: *augum, oh-am, oh-gum, oh-yam, and ach-ham,* among others; all are valid, depending on whether you ask someone from England, Ireland, Scotland, Wales, Brittany, or the many regions therein. The tree ogham is the best-survived set of teachings of this ancient system and is in use by a growing number of modern practitioners as a system of divination. There are many different associations with the ogham alphabet besides the trees; each letter also has other associations, such as bird ogham, color ogham, agricultural ogham, man ogham, woman ogham, king ogham, and many others. As for this oracle system, we will be working with the tree associations, as getting into the numerous other associations would lend itself to volumes of text far too convoluted to be useful as a modern oracle system.

The ancient Celts, specifically those of the druid orders, used this simple alphabet as a system for teaching their spoken traditions. Apprentice druids studied the ogham for years as part of their extensive training. All over the Celtic areas, there are still many stone markers with personal names carved on them that are believed to have been used for marking graves and land borders. Most examples of the ogham are from the fourth to the eighth centuries. There are textual references of the use of oghams carved on wood, but only stone examples remain today. Of the druids, we know that writing the knowledge of their teachings was forbidden. Due to this taboo, most of the historical writings about them are secondhand; however, from those writings we have discovered that each ogham is a simple mark used to embody an entire teaching. Although we think of the ogham today as an alphabet, it was believed to have been used also as a simple symbol to relate to a very in-depth teaching that would have been memorized and passed on orally. The ogham would simply be a mnemonic trigger for the entire teaching. It is also believed that the druid orders had a system of hand gestures that related to the ogham as well, so they were able to say one thing verbally and communicate something different with the secret language, the hand gesture, at the same time.

Ogham Letter	Celtic Name	Tree Associated	Key Words for Divination
B	Beith	Birch	Growth/Beginnings
L	Luis	Rowan	Protection/Defense
F	Fearn	Alder	Oracle/Teacher
S	Saille	Willow	Intuition/The Unseen
N	Nuin	Ash	Transformation/Action
H	Huath	Hawthorn	Obstacle/Tension
D	Duir	Oak	Strength/Endurance
T	Tinne	Holly	Challenge/Justice
C	Coll	Hazel	Inspiration/Wisdom
Q	Quert	Apple	Choice/Healing
M	Muin	Vine	Completion/Harvest
G	Gort	Ivy	Tenacity/Self
NG	Ngetal	Broom/Reed	Cleansing/Vitality
ST	Straif	Blackthorn	Adversity/Sacrifice
R	Ruis	Elder	Consequence/Regret
A	Ailim	Silverfir/Elm	Delight/Awe
O	Ohn	Gorse	Passion/Strength
U	Ur	Heather	Transition/Partnership
E	Eadha	Aspen	Courage/Steadfastness
I	Idho	Yew	Gateway/Mortality
CH	Koad	Grove	Oneness/Consciousness
TH	Oir	Spindle	Obligation/Discipline
PE	Iphin	Gooseberry	Comfort/Success
PH	Uilleand	Woodbine	Clarity/Focus
XI-AE	Phagos	Beech	Experience/Opportunity

The most ancient ogham examples are composed of a vertical center line, called a *druim,* intersected by various numbers of slashed lines of different angles. When it was written vertically, the ogham was read from the bottom up. An inverted *V* shape, or "feathered arrow," often appeared at the bottom of the druim line to show the beginning of the line. If they are written horizontally, as in the many early manuscripts that reference the ogham, they are read from left to right.

Ꭰow Scands che Foresc?

The tree ogham assigns different ranks of trees: chieftains, peasants, and shrubs. These ranks were descriptive of each tree's symbolic importance to the druids, bards, and ovates, not necessarily the physical stature of the plant or tree. There are a few versions of the ranks of the trees, one of which was derived from the Brehon Laws, which divided the trees according to the tree's uses and the penalties for felling the trees unlawfully.

The ogham is further grouped into four *aicmi,* or "tribes," of five letters, or "fews," each. The first three tribes are consonants. The B-tribe fews—B, L, F, S, and N—are all marked with strokes to the right of the center line, or druim. The H tribe—H, D, T, C, and Q—are all marked to the left of the druim line. The M-tribe fews—M, G, NG, ST, and R—are diagonal to the druim line. The A-tribe fews are the vowels A, O, U, E, and I, which all cross at a right angle through the middle of the druim. Five more fews, known as the *forfedha,* were added later to the ogham and are shown in *The Book of Ballymote*, a fourteenth-century text recording Irish sagas, laws, and genealogies that documents a key to the ogham. It is supposed that these fews were added when the Celts encountered other European cultures and began interacting and trading with them. These forfedha represent the diphthongs that had to be added to their language in order to communicate with these cultures, and these new sounds were eventually adopted by the Celts. The forfedha in this deck include CH, TH, PE, PH, and XI, and they are represented by various symbols that are obviously quite different from the original twenty fews. It should be noted that there are several versions of the forfedha, further suggesting that they were added later. After much study and comparison, I finally made the decision on what versions of the forfedha to use based on how well they would work for divination purposes. The twenty-five ogham fews included in this oracle deck are rendered as they appear in *The Book of Ballymote* and are illustrated as part of the back design of each card, as well as a Celtic knot tree depicted in its four seasons (see opposite page). As we do a reading, the seasonal trees remind us that everything happens in its turn and that it's our fate to remain as part of the cycles of life. The circular figure in the middle, known as Fionn's Window, is a reminder of the magical origins of this system and its proud continuance into the future.

While the origins of the ogham are unknown, many speculations abound. Some say they were developed to mimic the Roman letter system or were inspired by the Viking runes. According to Irish myths, Ogma, who was a chief of the

mysterious Tuatha de Danann, is credited as the inventor of the ogham alphabet. Ogma, also known as Ogma Sun Face, was a Celtic hero referred to as the Celtic Hercules. There is very little written about the myths of Ogma. We do know he was a warrior poet who carried a club and a sword, and was known for his eloquence (he has been referred to as "honey tongued").

Ogma is also mentioned in the stories of the magical crane-skin bag believed to hold secret wisdom. It is of interest that in *Vita Merlini* (Life of Merlin) by Geoffrey of Monmouth, several chiefs describe the flight of cranes as forming letters in the sky, as their flight was "in a curved line in the shape of certain letters." Anyone who has seen a crane fly will notice that its legs drag behind it, much like the slashes of the ogham letters. Robert Graves wrote that he believed the crane-skin bag was the vessel that held the secrets of the ogham.

According to legend, the sea god Manannan mac Lir owned the original crane bag. It was referred to as "a treasure of powers, with many virtues." He appeared to the sun god Lugh disguised as a warrior and gifted the bag to him. Lugh, incidentally, was the first person to receive a message written in ogham; because of the message, he was able to protect his wife from abduction. Lugh passed the crane bag to the three sons of Cermait Honeymouth (another name for Ogma). The bag finally ended up back with Manannan mac Lir. The secrets of the crane bag were passed around in this way. Today, those who use ogham staves as a divination and sacred tool often keep them in a cloth or leather bag, representing the original crane bag.

What Awaits You on This Journey

In the sections on each tree, you will find the Celtic name's pronunciation and definition; some of the ogham few's names actually translate as the name of the tree, but many translate into other words. Then I've included the status, letter, divinatory meaning, reversed meaning, tree symbolism and folk-lore, and physical information about the tree in a field guide section. I've also included a divining charm for each card; these charms were written based on the divinatory meanings of each card and on the classic poetic references known as the word oghams of Cuchulainn, Morrain mac Moin, and Oengus. The divining charms were designed to add meaning and further aid in understanding the symbolism of the cards. These poetic references enhance the connections to the sacred oral traditions and may be used in deeper meditations upon the ogham.

I have included the last five oghams, known as the forfedha, in this oracle system, because I believe they further contribute to the readings, but it's left up to the individual's choice whether to use them or not. Some ogham purists prefer not use these last five symbols. For those who only want to use the original, older twenty-symbol ogham system, you may simply leave the forfedha cards—grove, spindle, gooseberry, woodbine, and beech—out of the deck. In addition, it should be said that there are a few variations of interpretations of the ogham meanings in both historical and recent texts. I had to discover the meanings that rang true to me through my extensive literary and spiritual research on the topic, occasionally ironing out discrepancies I found by simply listening to the tree energies. In the event that you have worked with the ogham in the past and have learned interpretations that you prefer, by all means, feel free to apply those in your readings.

Included in this system are card layouts to help guide your way through the forest. You may use these layouts to do divinatory readings for yourself and others. You'll notice I've included the straightforward divinatory meanings for readings and additional messages for reversals (upside-down cards) if you choose to use them. If you don't want to read reversed cards, simply turn them all right-side up; the choice is entirely yours.

You will also learn other ways to use this deck to connect with the energies of the trees and the connected teachings of the ogham. You will discover how these cards can also be used as powerful meditation tools for self-transformation and discovery. Through this deck, you can journey through the sacred grove, where you will experience each card as part of a passage through the ogham. You will also learn ways to use these cards individually or in combination for some simple rituals to incorporate specific tree energies to achieve positive goals. I will also offer suggestions for creating your own affirmations and ways to incorporate tree magic and lore into your everyday life.

Turn the page and feel the breeze on your skin, smell the earth beneath your feet, and step into the green wood of an older time, when the trees were a part of us all.

Chapter 1

how to Use This Oracle

When you open your new ogham deck and flip through it, pay attention to how each image makes you feel. Notice the expressions, stances, and gestures of the people within this world of the ogham, as well as the colors, dynamic motion, and overall feel of each card. You'll also see that each card has the associated ogham and tree names at the top. At the bottom, keywords have been added to further jumpstart your card readings. After your initial examination of the cards, it's a good idea to go through this book and read the entry for each card. This way, you'll learn more about the mythic symbols on the cards and gain insight about each image of ogham lore.

Reading the Messages of the Trees

A reading with any oracle system is a picture of the energies that are aligning in the querent's life at the time of the reading. If I were giving you a reading, I'd tell you that the cards create a map of where you are, where you've been, and where you are likely to end up if you remain on your current path. The process of doing a reading brings awareness of the situation as a whole. A reading helps you access everything at your disposal—all the energies around you—in order to steer your life in the direction that you choose, even to the point of changing your outcome if you don't like where the current road is leading.

An oracle is a wonderful way to gain insight and an overview of a given situation. For these reasons, I don't really use the term *fortunetelling*, because nothing of the future is set in stone; while fate may guide us, our choices are our own. The concept of a changeable future outcome can become especially apparent while working with the ogham, because it is a system rooted in the folklore of the trees. Trees grow, change, and are as mutable as our destinies are; adjusting to the changing seasons without fear or pride, they simply *are*. This makes the ogham a wonderful system to work with, and with this deck, it is one you can readily learn and apply. Further on in this book, you will find card layouts designed for doing readings with this deck, or feel free to use other layouts of your choice or of your own design.

Dedicating the Cards

To begin, taking a deep breath, just relax and allow your energies to align with those of the cards. Take the cards in your hands and allow the voices of the forest of trees that you hold to whisper to you. Listen with your heart and soul. They speak of the very mysteries of birth, life, love, wisdom, death, and rebirth. If you try to hear them all at once, it may come to you in a rush, difficult to decipher—after all, sometimes it's hard to see the forest for the trees. So allow each tree to speak to you one by one, as each has its lesson.

Sit in a quiet place; under a tree is ideal, but indoors is fine too. If your cards are not in order, put them in order and place them before you. Light a stick of incense of your choice—sandalwood, frankincense, or a natural, woodsy scent would be good choices—just make sure it's a scent you like.

Hold up the first card, beith/birch, and look at the symbolism on the card. As you look at it, remember that each card is infused with tree energy, as I explained on page xvi. In doing this, I have placed in your hands something more than a stack of cards; rather, it is a powerful divination tool and a magical tool of transformation! You may now access that energy—open yourself up to it. As you look at the card, ask it to speak to you with the following charm:

> *Birch that grows from the earth below*
> *Speak to me that I will know.*

Awaken the energy by passing the card through the incense smoke, then holding it briefly to your forehead, and then to your heart. Follow the technique with each of the cards in turn (changing the name of the tree in the charm to match the card you are looking at, of course) until you have blessed the entire deck. Once you have completed each card, take the stack of cards in your hands and hold the deck to your forehead and then to your heart. Complete this dedication ritual with the following statement:

> *This deck I dedicate with mind and heart*
> *Both as a grove and each small part*
> *May it be a guide to me and mine*
> *By shrub, leaf, blossom, tree, and vine.*

Your cards are now dedicated to your use for divination, magic, learning, and meditation. You might wish to occasionally pass them through some incense smoke to cleanse them of any residual negativity from regular use. If other people handle your cards, the cards may begin to absorb energies of others that might not align with your intentions; if this happens, simply cleanse them in smoke again.

Making and Dedicating the Crane Bag

As we previously discussed, Manannan mac Lir, the sea god, was the original owner of the mythical crane-skin bag, which was believed to hold the secrets of the ogham. How did he come to possess such an extraordinary gift?

According to the legend, Aoife loved Manannan mac Lir's son, Ilbrach. She was tricked by a competitor for Ilbrach's attention to come into the water, where a dark enchantment

was cast upon her, turning her into a crane. The crane was a sacred totem animal of Manannan mac Lir; in some stories, he cared for her during her unfortunate enchantment. When Aoife finally died, she instructed Manannan to turn her crane hide into a magical bag that would hold great treasures. When the tide was high, all the treasures would be visible, but when it ebbed, the bag appeared to be empty. As the bag passed from one owner to another through the years, it became the legend that the original ogham and all its wisdom was kept within the bag.

The idea of the crane bag has been an important part of Celtic mythology and druid traditions. In modern druidry, many use a bag symbolically representing the crane bag to hold their most magical belongings. You may find a bag to serve as your crane bag for this grove of ogham cards, or make a bag yourself—traditionally white or green if it's made of cloth, although you may choose whatever fabric speaks to

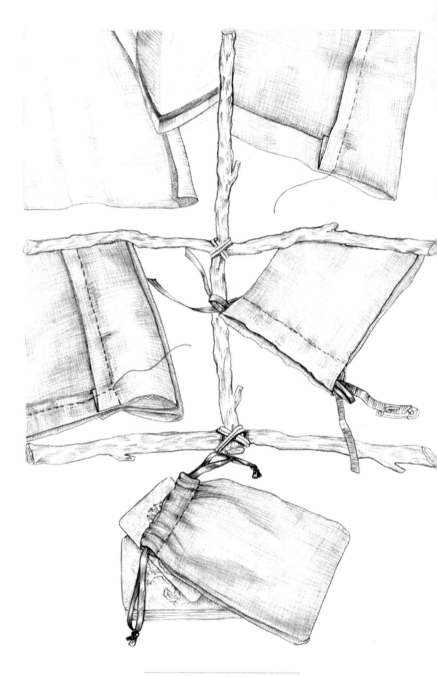

you, or it may be made of leather, but please respect the spirit of Aoife and do not harm a crane to make your bag.

You can make a simple bag yourself. For a basic cloth bag, you'll need:

- a piece of fabric 17 inches long by 6 inches wide
- 2 pieces of ¼-inch-wide ribbon, each 17 inches long
- an iron
- a safety pin
- a needle and thread or a sewing machine

Lay the fabric wrong-side up, fold the 17-inch sides in by a ½ inch, and press with an iron. Then fold the 6-inch side in by 1 inch and press with an iron. Stitch along the 1-inch fold you just made to form a channel that the ribbon drawstring will run through (see the top right illustration on the facing page). Fold the fabric in half, with the wrong side out (the side you want on the outside of your finished bag should be on the inside). Line up the top of the bag that you just stitched so that the edges are even. Starting where the stitching you just did ends, stitch along the side of the bag about ¼ inch from the edge, being careful not to stitch closed the channel for the ribbons to go through. Repeat on the other side.

Turn the bag right-side out. Now pin the safety pin to one end of a single piece of ribbon, close the safety pin, and use it to guide the ribbon through one side of the channel and continue through the other until both ends meet again. Tie the ribbon together. Repeat the process with the other ribbon, but begin on the opposite side of the bag—the ribbons will cross each other. When both ends of the second ribbon meet, tie those ends together as well. When you pull the knots, your new crane bag will close.

You may wish to decorate your bag using the Celtic crane symbol on page 15 or another symbol if you wish. You can add stone beads or feathers—be creative, and make it your own! When you're done personalizing your crane bag, you may wish to do a short dedication ritual using the following chant:

> *Within this crane bag oceans deep*
> *Holding knowledge I shall keep*
> *Within the bag my ogham grove*
> *This wisdom is my treasure trove*
> *By Aoife the Crane and Manannan mac Lir*
> *I dedicate this bag that holds treasures dear.*

You now have an enchanted bag to hold your ogham deck when it's not in use.

Chapter 2

A Field Guide to the Cards

By now, you have probably visited the images in this deck one by one. Did you notice that the people or animals in each image are interacting with the trees in different ways? All we see of the woman in the spindle card are her hands as they work. She can see the spindle tree outside of her workplace, signifying that her work is an important part of something bigger than herself. The man in the holly card seems to challenge you; the holly itself is a barrier as well. The woman in the willow card seems to be working together with the tree, drawing lunar, feminine energy from it. Ask yourself how each card makes you feel as you experience it. Chances are, your feelings while viewing each card are there for a reason.

These images are meant to evoke an emotional response, drawing you into the world of the Celtic trees and their vastly complex meanings. In this section of the book, you will find words to go along with these visual images, giving the emotional responses a more palpable meaning. The divining charm is a poetic gift from each tree, drawing upon the old teachings for each tree as well as each tree's traditional status. You'll learn the divinatory meanings to be used for a reading and the reversed meanings for cards that may end up upside down in a spread. You may choose to do your reading using these reversals, or simply flip all the cards right-side up if you prefer; the trees will leave it up to you to decide.

The descriptions of each image will point out some of the symbolism within the images; this should further help you make the connections between the meanings and the images. Folklore about each tree and its uses by humankind both ancient and modern can offer insight into the spirit of the trees and how they are part of our lives. Then, last but not least, you'll discover the field guide, offering botanical information about each tree's growth, environment, and propagation.

Combined, all of these bits of information will give you a basic lesson on each tree's individual personality and its effect on our lives, psyches, and spirits as you interpret the cards. The more you know about each tree, the more their voices will speak to you.

If you are ready, let us now step into the enchanted forest of the *Voice of the Trees*.

beith
BIRCH

Beith • Birch

Celtic Name: Beith (pronounced *beh*), "being"

Letter: B

Status: Peasant

Divining Charm

> *The beauty of youth brings strength to renew*
> *Treading the path with a partnership true*
> *Manifesting the future by brave work and plan*
> *Silver trunks soon beginning to strengthen the land.*

Divinatory Meaning: Growth, beginnings

The beith/birch card marks the beginning of the ogham journey. When this card comes up in a reading, it represents new beginnings and positive change—the fortuitous beginning of a new project. It can also be the beginning of a new cycle or a new work or romantic relationship. Now is the time to get into the proper frame of mind for success and start the groundwork and planning to achieve your goals. This is *your* groundbreaking! Be prepared and plan ahead.

Reversed Meaning

You may need to rethink the direction you have been going in. It's time to reinvent yourself; what has worked before will not work now—you need to allow yourself to blossom. Don't spend time dwelling on what has been destroyed in the past.

Now is the time to focus on what is beginning to grow out of the ashes of that loss, for it needs you to nurture it along.

Symbolism and Lore

Here is a boy of a Celtic tribe, his pony packed with birch saplings. They are a working partnership, assisting each other in both work and fellowship. The youth wears green and yellow, the colors of spring and growth. He has planned his venture, bringing along all the supplies he might need for his journey of planting new life. At his belt is a shovel, representing preparation to work hard toward goals. A bird soars overhead, pointing to joy and divine guidance.

Birches are known as "nursery trees"—after a forest fire, birches are the first trees to grow upon the cleared land, making a protected and nurtured environment for other species of trees to then take root. Birch is also one of the first trees in the spring to burst forth with leaves, reminding us of renewal and rebirth every year.

Birch was often the wood that became Maypoles in spring Beltane celebrations. Birch twigs were sometimes used for a besom, or broom, and are thus associated with the Goddess and magic. Another of birch's associations is that of love; the tree was often a meeting place for sweethearts, and wreaths of birch were considered a token of love. Qualities of love, protection, and inception make birch a popular choice for making cradles.

It may seem strange to many, but birch was also used in death rituals; its branches were an important part of the burial rites. The Celts saw death simply as a gateway into the next world, so birch would have been used as a way to usher in rebirth after death. The theme of renewal is also reflected in the practice of the use of birch branches for ritual purification. Druids used birch branches to drive out the spirits of the old year. Until fairly recent times, European prisoners underwent a practice known as "birching." They were whipped with birch branches in the belief that it would purify them. This practice would have been a holdover from times when people used birch branches to drive out the old and what no longer served in order to make way for spring and new life.

Field Guide

The silver birch (*Betula pendula*) is native to Europe and extends into Asia Minor. Downy birch (*Betula pubescens*) also grows throughout Europe and is common in Scotland. There are many varieties of birch all over North America.

Silver birch is a fast-growing deciduous tree reaching a height of up to almost one hundred feet but only living between sixty and ninety years. Its trunk is tall and slender, and the bark is white with black diamond-shaped patches. Many birch tree varieties have bark that peels off the trunk, but the silver birch's bark does not. Its leaves appear around April and are oval-shaped, toothed, and arranged alternately. Each birch tree produces both male and female flowers, called catkins, that appear at the same time as the leaves in spring and are pollinated by wind. Each female catkin produces hundreds of tiny winged seeds in late summer or early autumn that are dispersed by the wind. Only a few of those seeds will germinate and sprout. In the fall, the silver birch's leaves turn a bright yellow.

The birch has very long roots that tap into nutrients deep in the soil, depositing those nutrients in the autumn to the surface soil as it drops its leaves. It is considered a pioneer species, growing well on open ground and preparing the area for other plant life and trees to grow.

Luis • Rowan

Celtic Name: Luis (pronounced *lweesh*), "herb"

Letter: L

Status: Shrub

Divining Charm

Be you man or cattle, your strength is the same
The quicken tree fills you with wit and with flame
Be you warded and safe as you travel the land
Delighting the eye as protection's at hand.

Divinatory Meaning: Protection, defense

Rowan assures you that you are surrounded by protection from negativity, enchantments, or other danger. There may be forces attempting to thwart your efforts, but you are under a divine shield guarding you against their malice. Listen to your inner voice; it's guiding you to avoid pitfalls. You must pay attention to what is going on around you, but by activating your abilities and insight, you should have no trouble keeping your senses about you right now. You are strong, warded, feeling confident and safe; just remain aware, realizing that there may be trouble nearby, but it's easily avoidable. Any conflict you do encounter will be temporary.

Reversed Meaning

You must open your eyes to the dangers that are around you, taking the proper precautionary actions. You need to

luis
ROWAN

prevent outside forces from interfering with your actions right now. You may be feeling vulnerable currently; you are spreading yourself too thin. Focus on what you are doing and where you are going. Listen to your own inner voice.

Symbolism and Lore

The rowan tree has long been associated with magical protection, so the luis/rowan card is a good omen that you are warded by spirit. In this card, the traveler walks the countryside with his rowan staff in hand. It was believed that a rowan staff offered protection to travelers, and here the spirit of the rowan staff is revealed as an etheric dragon keeping watch over its ward. The traveler is confident that he is safe, and even though we notice a few dark-looking and possibly mischievous elementals nearby, they're recoiling from the powerful shielding magic of the rowan staff. The crane-skin bag at his hip represents his knowledge and a reminder that he values his own guidance and life lessons passed down from greater sources. As he passes by the rowan tree, he misses stepping into a nearby faerie ring marked by mushrooms, therefore avoiding otherworldly danger and possible detainment by the fae.

Rowan is a powerful protective amulet. The protective symbol of the star, or pentagram, appears on the end of the rowan berry. Songbirds love to eat the berries of the rowan tree, adding to its mystical connections to the otherworld. Rowan is associated with the goddess Brighid, music, poetry, fire, and protection. In older times, an equal-armed cross tied with red string or thread was hung upon doors and stables as a ward against dark magic. It was also hung on a baby's cradle to prevent the infant from being kidnapped by faeries and replaced by a changeling. Rowans are found growing near stone circles, other sacred sites, and along ley lines, probably to protect them from any malicious energy. Rowan trees are also associated with guardian dragon spirits, which, interestingly, are also tied in with ley lines.

According to legend, the Tuatha de Danann, the magical people of the goddess Danu, accidentally dropped a rowan berry when they passed through the woods. It grew into a quicken tree and was recognized as a druid tree grown from a berry of the Land of the Ever-Living Ones. It is known that the druids, to focus their magic for strength and protection for their people, made bonfires of rowan wood before important battles.

Field Guide

The rowan tree (*Sorbus aucparia*) is sometimes called mountain ash due to its similar leaves, but it's not a member of the ash family; it is in the family Rosaceae. Rowan is found all over Europe and in western Asia, Russia, and Morocco. Its close cousin, American mountain ash (*Sorbus americana*), grows in many areas of North America. Rowan grows in a variety of elevations but is often found in the mountains. The rowan can grow up to sixty feet tall but is usually smaller. Its bark is smooth and gray, sometimes almost a purplish color, with dark, raised spots across it. Its leaves are oval-shaped matched pairs, or pinnate, along a thin stalk, with a terminal leaflet at the end. Rowan is a deciduous tree whose leaves appear in April. In May, the rowan becomes covered with clusters of white blossoms whose strong, sweet scent attracts many insects, such as bees and beetles, that pollinate the flowers. In August, the fertilized flowers set and ripen into small red-orange berries with a pentagram symbol at the base. The berries are a feast for many birds, who then scatter the seeds. Rowan berries have a bitter flavor but are edible and rich in vitamin C. They can be cooked with other fruits and made into preserves or pies.

fearn
ALDER

Fearn • Alder

Celtic Name: Fearn (pronounced *FAIRn*), "alder"

Letter: F

Status: Chieftain

Divining Charm

Oracle wisdom like milk flowing down
Shields your position like the tooth of a hound
In your quest of the spiritual warrior, be wise
Shield your emotions while you heed good advice.

Divinatory Meaning: Oracle, teacher

Alder is the blessed tree that speaks to you of your own inner teacher as well as taking the good advice of a sage. Now is the time to be open to the counsel of a teacher or mentor, as well as your spirit guides. While seeking knowledge, don't discount your own wise counsel. A spiritual warrior is wise enough to seek inspiration and listen carefully to the advice of others, weighing all options thoughtfully in order to triumph. Use your own judgment, exploring all possibilities before acting on advice. Often, you will find the answers you need when you connect with the sage within you.

Reversed Meaning

You may be closing yourself off to good advice that is being offered; reexamine the counsel of others that you may have discounted. Right now you need to shield yourself from making decisions based solely on emotion. Look at the situation from a new perspective and apply logic, allowing yourself to be open to the advice of others. Combine that with your inner wisdom to find a solution.

Symbolism and Lore

The alder tree is the sacred tree of the Celtic hero Bran the Blessed. Bran was a great king in Celtic legend. A giant of a man, he was a great warrior, wise and magical. Bran is considered a brother to the alder, as if they are one in spirit. One legend tells how Bran was mortally injured in battle, but due to the powers of the goddess Rhiannon's magical birds, his head remained alive for seven years and acted as an oracle. Eventually, the head became silent and was buried on the White Hill, where it is believed that the Tower of London stands. Bran's head still guards London to this day.

Bran is seen on this card meditating beneath an alder tree surrounded by water. The rain falling from the sky is no distraction, as he keeps his own counsel; his alder shield protects him from the water's emotional influence. He remains prepared to take decisive action; his sword is ready at his side. He wears garments dyed from alder—the bark makes a red dye for both red and black wool, the young shoots make a yellow dye, and the older shoots produce a tawny shade. His spirit animal, the raven, keeps watch over him as he communes with his inner sage.

Alder has many interesting properties, one of which is its water-resistant ability. This made it a good choice for milk buckets and other liquid-holding vessels and ancient bridges.

The Celts used several woods for making shields, and the alder was one of them. Alder was considered a sacred tree for many reasons; one was that when it was cut, the wood would begin to turn red, as if it were bleeding like a human. Alder was also used in weather magic; the pith was pushed out of a small twig of alder, and it was said witches used such a whistle to "whistle up the wind."

Field Guide

The alder tree (*Alnus glutinosa*) is known as king of the waters. It thrives in moist soil, loves to grow near water, and is native to most of Europe but will grow in zones 3–7 of the United States as well. As a member of the birch family, alder shares its beneficial properties—it also will grow well in damaged areas that have been burned or have acidic soil, healing the earth it grows in by adding nitrogen to the soil. The European alder can reach heights of nearly one hundred feet.

The alder is a deciduous tree that has simple and broad, serrated leaves that turn warm colors in the fall. It reproduces by elongated male catkins and shorter woody female catkins opening in the early spring, often before the leaves appear. The alder is self-pollinating, primarily by wind but with a little help from bees as well. The female catkins look like cones that open and disperse seeds upon maturity. This is a fast-growing tree and is often used as a windbreak in Scotland, sheltering gardens from high winds.

Alder wood has a lovely reddish hue similar to that of cedar and has proven itself useful through the ages. In addition to the Celts' use of alder for shields, milk buckets, and many shades of dye, it is used in various modern products as well, including furniture, cabinetry, woodchips for smoking fish and meat, artist's charcoal, and as one of the woods used for electric guitar bodies.

Saille • Willow

Celtic Name: Saille (pronounced *SAHL-yuh*), "willow"

Letter: S

Status: Peasant

Divining Charm

Otherworld influence is guiding your aims
The white, cold moon as it waxes and wanes
With the strength of bees that whisper to you
Guided by intuition in all that you do.

Divinatory Meaning: Intuition, the unseen

The willow card's message is to follow your intuition, to work harmoniously within the cycles of events instead of trying to fight against them. Lunar influences of love and emotion are strong in your life right now; you are emotionally sensitive at this time. There may be unseen forces at work, so be aware that you may not know the entire situation; therefore, you may be unable to act until you have all the information. Pay particular attention to your dreams, for magical powers are at hand and may try to assist you through dreams. The realms of spirit are wide open to you right now; you are feeling a deep communing with your higher power.

saille
WILLOW

Reversed Meaning

You may be overwhelmed with emotion right now, having trouble separating fantasy from reality. You need to push your roots down deep and perhaps back away from a situation in order to get your bearings and successfully find balance between the spiritual and mundane worlds. Remember, it is often better to bend in the wind like a willow than to try to be so rigid that you crack under pressure.

Symbolism and Lore

The white willow tree of the Celtic lands, as well as every other willow, is traditionally a goddess tree, linked with the powers of the moon cycles, water, intuition, divination, and magic. The willow is a sacred tree of the druids and was revered in old Irish law as well. Celtic goddesses Cerridwen and Arianrhod are associated with the willow tree, as are many goddesses of divination and the underworld from other pantheons.

The priestess in the willow card blesses a scrying bowl of water beneath a willow tree on a full moon night. She hears the beating wings of an owl, a sacred symbol of the wisdom of the White Goddess; it acts as a reminder that her higher power guides her. She will peer into the scrying bowl to find the answers to what is unseen in order to better choose her course of action. As she connects to the goddess power of the willow and the full moon, she remains rooted to the earth, holding balance between the realms.

There are many varieties of willows throughout the world. The graceful weeping willow, which is a popular ornamental tree in the United States, carries some of the white willow's DNA in its essence; it is actually a hybrid of white willow and the Peking willow. Young willow stems are very flexible and are used in basketmaking; traditionally, these flexible shoots were also used to secure birch branches in brooms. Dowsers, or "water witches," find the willow's branches particularly useful when dowsing for water. It is also one of many woods used in making wands.

Field Guide

The white willow tree (*Salix alba*) is native to Europe and western and central Asia, and will grow in zones 2–8 of the United States. The white willow is a deciduous tree that grows between thirty and ninety feet tall. Its bark is grayish brown and becomes very rough as the tree matures. Its stalks and leaves droop downward, but not as dramatically as the weeping willow. The leaves are thin and bladelike, finely toothed, and arranged alternately on a long stem. The white willow's leaves are paler when compared to its cousin willows and are covered on the underside with silvery, silken hairs. The white willow is dioecious; both male and female trees each produce catkins in the spring. They are usually pollinated by bees and other insects, and both a male and a female tree are needed to produce seeds.

It digs its roots down deep in damp soil, where it loves to grow; sunny areas with bad drainage or even occasional flooding will support a willow nicely. Willow, like alder, is used in making artist's drawing charcoal. The white willow specifically is a source of salicylic acid, which is derived from its bark. Salicylic acid is the precursor to aspirin, which made white willow bark an indispensable pain reliever and fever reducer in the ancient world.

nuin
ASH

Nuin • Ash

Celtic Name: Nuin (pronounced *NEE-uhn*), "letter"

Letter: N

Status: Peasant

Divining Charm

> *She boasted upon him, a warrior strong*
> *To sharpen his steel, to face down the throng*
> *Now peace must be checked, there's action to take*
> *Like the strength of the sun that appears at daybreak.*

Divinatory Meaning: Transformation, action

It will take strong action to break the inertia that is affecting you right now. Sometimes it's best to play along and do your best to keep the peace, but this is not that time. Often, you need to create a little friction or even face a conflict in order to grow, and this is the message that the ash card has for you. You have planned as much as you can; now it's time to go into the situation at hand and take care of business. Facing a challenging situation will transform you and help you forge a new reality.

Reversed Meaning

You may be in a situation where you are frustrated by feeling like you have a lack of control over how things are going. If you are concerned about risks involved in taking action, remember there is often more to risk in the future by standing by and doing nothing, however easier that may be. Do not allow yourself to become a pawn; if you have been waiting to take action until the time is right, this is your wake-up call.

Symbolism and Lore

The ash tree is part of the magical triumvirate of the faerie grove: oak, ash, and thorn. Ash is a tree that is steeped in myth; it was believed by the Norse to be the world tree Yggdrasil. The sun god, Lugh, was described as bearing a magical spear of ash wood called Millar. It was said that no battle could be sustained against it or against the man who held it. One of Lugh's titles was Lugh of the Long Arm, possibly suggesting the spear as part of him.

Here, on the ash card, we see Lugh with the sun shining on his shoulders through a mighty ash tree. He wears woad war paint as he sharpens his bronze spearhead with a stone, preparing to decisively face a conflict head-on. Lugh has many talents—among them blacksmith, cup bearer, bard, wheelwright, hero, historian, poet, harper, craftsman, sorcerer, and warrior. Lugh is truly a man of action, and his action is backed by wisdom. As he sharpens his spear, focusing upon his goals, he breaks inertia and knows that the initiative he takes will bravely bring about change in the world. On a spiritual level, he is aware that in order to make the music and write the poetry that he loves, he must sometimes boldly shake things up and fight for what is needed to protect these things in life. In addition to its popularity with the Celts for making spears, the ash was also the wood of choice among many fletchers for making arrows.

Field Guide

The European or common ash (*Fraxinus excelsior*) is native to most of Europe and has quite a few close cousins in the United States, such as white ash, blue ash, and green ash. Ash is a deciduous tree with a tall, domed crown. They commonly are around fifty to seventy feet tall, and some of the oldest are around 250 years old. Its bark is smooth on young trees, becoming darker and rougher with age, bearing many furrows and ridges. Its leaves are some of the last to open in spring and are pinnate, compound leaves with seven to thirteen broad, serrated leaflets.

Most trees have either male or female flowers (and can switch from year to year); only occasionally will one tree have both. The tiny bunches of flowers are dark purple, without petals; the females' are slightly longer than the males' and are pollinated by the wind. European ash has less than remarkable autumn coloring and is one of the first trees to drop its leaves. Sometimes the ash drops dull green leaves, leaving behind bunches of long, winged seeds that stay on the tree during the winter. These are referred to as ash keys; it is said that carrying one in your pocket is a powerful protection against enchantments. Green ash keys harvested in the early summer can also be pickled and eaten.

Ash wood is commonly used to make many items that point to its association with taking action, energy, and transformation, as well as with Lugh and his many talents: baseball bats, tool handles, hockey sticks, smoking chips, flooring, and oars are just a few.

huath
HAWTHORN

Ⱨuaⱦ · Ⱨawⱦoᴙn

Celtic Name: Huath (pronounced *HOO-ah*), "terror"

Letter: H

Status: Peasant

Divining Charm

> *A pack of wolves by tooth and claw*
> *Brings fear of harm, your sword to draw*
> *Do not pale, you may stand or take flight*
> *The sun will rise after a difficult night.*

Divinatory Meaning: Obstacle, tension

Hawthorn warns of a brief period of tension in your path. Whether financial, personal, or romantic issues, you will likely face some disruptions and anxiety while trying to reach your goals. They will seem like greater difficulties than they really are; just watch your back and be careful. Don't allow depression to set in because things aren't going your way; fear will only make good judgment difficult and become a chink in your armor. You must act with wisdom, and you may need to wait out the situation rather than act rashly. You may be facing a test and be in a situation where applying force won't solve your problems. There are no shortcuts, but if you work through it with finesse, this time of difficulty will bring a rosy outcome.

Reversed Meaning

You may find yourself up against an impassable barrier. You have to know when to fight it out and when to count your losses and change course before more damage is done. No one likes to give in, but sometimes it's better to protect what you have left after a skirmish and take the lessons you've learned from it, surviving to fight the next battle.

Symbolism and Lore

A warrior is traveling alone; he may be on his way to meet his comrades or on his way home to his lass after the battle. Although he is armed, he senses a difficult obstacle on his journey: a pack of wolves that he has heard in the distance. They are tracking something in the woods. Knowing that he is one man against perhaps a dozen sets of hungry fangs, he takes refuge off the trail, beneath a hawthorn tree. Poised and ready to strike if he needs to, he sees them race past and realizes that he made the right decision—they are after another quarry. If he can remain still and quiet, and in control of his own fear, he may come out of this without a scratch and wiser for it.

Hawthorn, sometimes known as whitethorn, is one-third of the triad of faerie trees: oak, ash, and thorn. Its blossoms are white and its berries are red—the colors associated with the Celtic underworld and the realm of the fae. Hawthorn was often used in hedgerows, its thorny branches making a strong barrier. Hawthorn can be considered a magical barrier against psychic attack as well. There are many superstitions surrounding the hawthorn; there have been occasions of construction plans being changed in the British Isles out of fear of destroying a hawthorn believed to be enchanted. Hawthorn is also associated with Beltane or May Day. Hawthorn blossoms are an important part of these celebrations and are traditional decorations for Maypoles.

Field Guide

Crataegus monogyna is just one of the numerous genus and species of the hawthorn. Native to Europe, hawthorns are grown as individual trees and also as hedgerows. When not pruned back into hedgerows, a hawthorn tree grows to about nineteen feet tall and just about as wide. This deciduous tree has brown bark with gray tones, is rough and slightly scaly in texture, and is covered in sharp, hard thorns. Its leaves are alternate, simple, and toothed; most hawthorns have deeply lobed leaves, but they vary from species to species.

In May, the hawthorn produces lovely white blossoms with five petals each and bright pink anthers (the pollen-bearing part of a stamen). They are pollinated by many insects, including flies. When in bloom, the hawthorn has a very rich scent, and whether it is pleasant or not seems to be a matter of opinion. While some find the scent sweet or sexy, many others discern the beginning stages of putrefaction in its perfume, which actually attracts flies to pollinate the tree.

All summer, the fruit of the hawthorn develops, ripening in the fall. The berries, called haws, are enjoyed by many varieties of birds, who spread the seed by dropping them in their travels. The hawthorn has many uses: the blossoms, leaves, and berries are all edible, and the berries have numerous medicinal uses as well.

Varieties of hawthorn are found all over Europe and North America. They will grow well in most soils and are happy even in partial shade. They don't have very large root balls and don't overfeed on the nutrients in the surrounding soil either. These hardy trees have been known to live for over four hundred years.

Duir · Oak

Celtic Name: Duir (pronounced *DOO-r*), "oak"

Letter: D

Status: Chieftain

Divining Charm

You have done good work upon a bended knee
A doorway before you, bright and shining with ease
The highest of bushes affords strength and security
Your work will endure both with honor and surety.

Divinatory Meaning: Strength, endurance

A doorway stands before you; it's a clear sign of a passageway to a higher place of status, both in a physical and a spiritual sense. You're coming into your own strength. Your roots run deep with experience, and all the trials you have been through so far have helped you establish your position. You may have found that you've become a sheltering force to others as well, respected for your credibility, with people coming to you for advice based upon your experience of opening doors for others. If you're working on a project currently, signs point to its success as long as you stand your ground when needed.

Reversed Meaning

Be careful that you honorably use the power that is placed in your hands. You've been called upon as a person of status, and others rely on your good judgment. Now is the time to

duir
OAK

examine your own motives and make sure that you are acting for the good of everyone involved, not just for your own gain. Like it or not, you're respected, and with that comes a great responsibility.

Symbolism and Lore

A rutting stag trumpets his voice through the woods. Before him stands a grand and ancient oak tree, enduring through the ages. Wind, ice, and even lightning strikes have been a part of the existence of this behemoth, and still it stands, strong and noble, its roots running deep into the earth. A doorway seems to have appeared beneath one of its low-hanging boughs; aglow with the light of the afternoon sun, it creates a symbolic portal. This is not a passage into another world but a symbolic doorway to another stage of your own life; if you choose to enter, you will find great honors and equal responsibilities.

Along with ash and thorn, the oak is one of the three sacred faerie trees and is also sacred to the Dagda, the ancient god and high king of the Tuatha de Danann. The Dagda is a very old, primal entity. He is very much rooted in the physical realm, a tough-as-nails party animal you could count on in a pinch; one of his symbols is a rutting stag. The Dagda also possessed a cauldron that could bring the dead back to life as well as offer a bottomless feast that left no man unsatisfied. In the ogham, the Dagda's association with the oak is all about strength, generosity, and kingship.

To the Celts, the oak was a very important tree long associated with the concept of the connection between the high king and the prosperity of the land. Many of the animals the Celts hunted also fed on acorns, and when they began to domesticate pigs, they fed on acorns as well; therefore, the oak was an important bringer of abundance. Acorns could be boiled and mashed, offering sustenance to people. It was also said that the druids, to draw in power, would chew on an acorn before prophesying. Druids would often gather in oak groves for their rites. Oak trees are often the target of lightning strikes but seem to have an excellent survival rate from such onslaughts, making them seem very godlike indeed.

Field Guide

Quercus robur is the mighty English oak. There are hundreds of oak species all over Europe, the Americas, and Asia. The oak is a large deciduous tree that can grow to about a hundred feet tall. They can live for a very long time; many old oaks are hundreds of years old, and some are reported to be 1,500 years old, and even older. Its distinctive leaves are lobed, very short-stalked, and arranged spirally on its branches. Oaks have smooth, brownish-gray bark when young, but the bark becomes very rough as they age. They produce catkin flowers in the spring and are pollinated by wind; oaks can be pollinated by other species within the *Quercus* genus, leading to much hybridization among them. In the midsummer, acorns begin to appear, each usually containing one seed and ripening in the autumn. The English oak produces acorns about one inch long, although different species have varying sizes of acorns. They are held by a cuplike structure, called a cupule, with one to four acorns on each stalk.

Oak is resistant to fungus because of its high tannin content, and it is an excellent wood for many kinds of woodworking. It's prized for wood floors, furniture, and building timber, and, yes, oak doors. Oak is a popular choice for barrels used in making wine, scotch, and bourbon. Oak woodchips are used for smoking foods such as fish and cheeses.

tinne
HOLLY

Tinne · Holly

Celtic Name: Tinne (pronounced *CHIN-yuh*), "iron"

Letter: T

Status: Shrub

Divining Charm

Holly warns of challenges coming your way
The wheels are turning, the weapons at play
Remain strong and brave as you walk through the fire
May the flames of attack strengthen you like iron.

Divinatory Meaning: Challenge, justice

Challenges are ahead. You will be tested, face difficult trials, or find yourself in a situation where justice will be served one way or another. The challenge placed in your path will test you to your limits; how you face that test is entirely up to you. You will need to draw upon your knowledge and skills to remain balanced, but if you are willing to walk through the fire, you'll emerge with greater strength and wisdom than you had before. When the wood of holly is heated in the flames, it becomes tempered, hard as iron.

Reversed Meaning

You may be entering into a fight you can't win at this time. You may need to retreat for a time, gain more knowledge about the situation, and decide on your direction before you proceed. Finding balance will serve you well in your preparation.

Symbolism and Lore

The tinne/holly card portrays a challenger in your path. He wears greenish armor, showing a connection to the Green Knight, the mythic challenger of Sir Gawain of Arthurian legend. The Green Knight has strong ties to the holly; in addition to his axe, he carried a weapon of holly (either a spear or a club, depending upon the version of the legend). The mysterious Green Knight survives beheading, and the holly is evergreen, fully surviving winter, the season of death. The Green Knight returned to challenge Sir Gawain as a grim dealer of justice.

The helmet worn by the challenger in this card is reminiscent of the helmet found at the Sutton Hoo site, where a Saxon warrior had been buried. The Saxons were a real threat to the ancient Celtic tribes; many battles were fought between these two peoples that tested the steel of both. The flames on his brow represent the flames that temper and harden the holly, making it strong as iron. Beyond this immediate challenger, rocky cliffs are seen as a symbol that the way will not be easy, but green life grows from the cliffs as a reminder to keep hope alive.

The holly was reportedly one of the three woods used to make chariot wheels. *Táin Bó Cúailnge,* "The Cattle Raid of Cooley," points to holly being used in this way, as well as to make weapons. The Celtic hero Cuchulainn is described being attacked and stabbed by spears made of holly hardened in a fire.

You may notice that in the order of the ogham, holly follows oak. In folklore, the Oak King represents the summer solstice, the waxing half of the year, fruition, and bounty. The Holly King represents the winter solstice, the waning half of the year. The two brothers battle at the solstices, each taking over the rule from the other in his own time. For this reason, holly became associated with Christmas and Yule. The battle between the oak and holly kings has been carried on throughout the ages in the form of traditional folk-dancing processions such as morris dancing. The holly is also sometimes paired with ivy, another evergreen plant. In the Old English folk song, the holly is the masculine and the ivy is the feminine that face off in a battle of the sexes.

Field Guide

English holly (*Ilex aquifolium*) is native to the British Isles and southern and central Europe, although there are many varieties of holly that can be found all over the world. Most holly trees are tamed and trimmed into hedges or ornamental bushes, but when left to grow naturally, they become large trees—up to sixty-five feet in height. They are large, dense, and slow-growing trees or shrubs that can either grow alone or as a hedge. The holly is a broadleaf evergreen with one-to three-inch thick, waxy, spiny leaves of a dark green hue. New bark is green and smooth, but the older bark is gray and rougher. The wood is whitish green and very hard and dense. It is excellent for carving and for making furniture.

Holly trees are dioecious, which means there are both male and female plants; both have tiny, sweetly scented white flowers in May and June and are pollinated by bees. The female plant bears berries in the autumn, which remain all winter. Holly berries grow in loose clusters and range in color from orange to bright red; they are enjoyed as a delicacy by birds but are poisonous to humans. Holly trees spread by the dispersal of berries by birds and also by suckering and layering. Holly trees thrive in shade or sun, in well-drained, slightly acidic soil.

Coll · Hazel

Celtic Name: Coll (pronounced *cull*), "hazel"

Letter: C

Status: Chieftain

Divining Charm

> *The sweetest of woods and the hazel wood's duty*
> *The fairest of trees to its wood owes its beauty*
> *In the hazelnut find inspiration's bright kingdom*
> *Nine nuts from the hazel fed the Salmon of Wisdom.*

Divinatory Meaning: Inspiration, wisdom

Inspiration from a higher source will be bestowed upon you, as the hazel feeds you with spiritual nourishment. You are at a creative high point. Everything will proceed smoothly if you trust your intuition and proceed bravely, with the knowledge that all will go according to plan. Through your apprenticeship, you're discovering your own power. Sometimes you'll need to act quickly and change your plan as you go along, but you have all the wisdom, energy, and inspiration that you need to dance through situations with grace and power. This card also indicates that you may end up as a referee in some kind of conflict; trust in your own insight and wisdom, and you will settle the dispute fairly.

coll
HAZEL

Reversed Meaning

You may be experiencing a creative block or have feelings of disillusionment. You have become stagnant in your way of thinking and believe that your muse has abandoned you. You must overcome your fears and learn to trust your intuition in order to dissolve this block.

Symbolism and Lore

The coll/hazel card shows a hazel tree heavy with ripe hazelnuts on the bank of a river. A salmon leaps up out of the river to catch a falling hazelnut in its mouth. The hazelnut glows with the light of inspiration. Each time the Salmon of Wisdom eats a hazelnut, a spot appears on its side; it is about to consume the ninth and final magical hazelnut.

In one Celtic legend, according to a prophecy, a man named Finn would eat the Salmon of Wisdom and thereby gain its power. An old poet named Finegas had been trying to catch the mysterious salmon that lived in the Boinn River beneath the hazel tree, dining on hazelnuts. Believing that he could be the one destined to gain the wisdom, he stopped a traveling lad and asked for his help. The fish jumped out at the young man's feet. The traveler agreed to roast the fish for Finegas, who told him to be very careful not to taste even a small amount. As he roasted the fish, a blister rose up on the salmon's skin and the youth pushed it down with his thumb, burning himself. He immediately put his thumb into his mouth. He served the salmon to Finegas, who, knowing the power of the salmon was in the first taste of it, asked, "You didn't eat any, did you?" He told the old poet about his injury and his accidental taste of the fish. Old Finegas said, "Your name must be Finn!" The young man was indeed Finn Mac Cool (Fionn mac Cumhaill), who later became a great Irish hero known for his wisdom and gift of otherworldly knowledge. Whenever he wanted to access his divine gift of prophesy, he bit upon his thumb.

The hazel has been revered for its wonderful nuts, which have long been associated with wisdom, inspiration, and enlightenment. The hazel is the ninth tree in the ogham, and the salmon ate nine hazelnuts. Nine is a sacred number to the Celts, a number of enlightenment. Hazelnuts have been used for good luck, and hazel branches have been used as wands and dowsing rods.

Field Guide

The European hazel or common hazel (*Corylus avellana*) is a deciduous tree that's widely spread throughout much of Europe and North America and is a member of the birch family. It typically grows as an understory in deciduous forests, especially with oaks and conifers. Hazel trees prefer soil that is not acidic and are often found in low-lying areas. Hazel's not one of the largest trees, usually growing only about thirty feet in height if it is not pruned and left to grow wild; it generally lives fifty to seventy years. It grows bright green leaves upon its scaly, light umber–colored branches. The bark on older trees begins to peel. The tree usually has a number of trunks branching out from the ground that are the hosts of several rare and endangered lichens. The leaves of the hazel are fuzzy, with jagged edges, and grow up to four inches across.

In February, the hazel tree bursts forth with nearly two-inch-long male catkins and small female flowers of tufted red. They are fertilized by wind, but the hazel is self-incompatible, which means the pollen of a different hazel tree must fertilize the female buds.

Hazelnuts grow in clusters of three or four that ripen in September. The nuts of the hazel tree have an acornlike shape with reddish-brown shells, about three-fourths of an inch wide. Hazel trees feed people and many animals of the forest, including deer, mice, and squirrels.

quert
APPLE

Quert · Apple

Celtic Name: Quert (pronounced *kwairt*), "apple"

Letter: Q

Status: Peasant

Divining Charm

An excellent emblem in the apple you find
To heal your soul and bring peace of mind
Two beauties before you by your choice you must stand
The choice must be made by your very own hand.

Divinatory Meaning: Choice, healing

A choice between two equally beautiful things must be made. You find yourself in a period of rest and regeneration. You may be in need of emotional and spiritual healing; this is an opportunity to take time to relax and allow your body and spirit to build up your growing strength. This is a time of well-being, and you find yourself in a safe sanctuary. If you have been sick or going through a rough patch, this difficult cycle is coming to a close; your vitality is growing. You will be able to look back and see the way in which your challenges have made you stronger and thrive in new ways. The quert card can also represent a love affair where a choice must be made or a lover who will help you in your healing.

Reversed Meaning

You need to stop being indecisive and make a choice—either choice is good, but waiting is counterproductive to your best interests. Quert is a gentle warning that you need to take care of your personal energies and resources; you must take time out to nurture yourself or allow yourself to be nurtured.

Symbolism and Lore

On the quert/apple card, we see a priestess of Avalon in a sacred apple grove at the foot of Glastonbury Tor. Glastonbury is the location most often associated with the legend of Avalon. The priestess presents you with two apples, both beautiful, and you may choose one. This is a place of sanctuary and healing, where you feel at peace and find regeneration. You will notice that near the few image on the card, an apple is shown cut horizontally. When an apple is cut in this way, it shows the seeds forming a star pattern, which, encircled in the apple, represents the pentagram. This star pattern is repeated throughout nature and is an emblem of protection, spiritual shielding, and the earth element.

The apple tree and its fruit are associated with health and well-being. This is reflected in the old saying "An apple a day keeps the doctor away." Avalon is one of the Celtic names for the otherworld; it literally means "the isle of apples." Avalon is, of course, the place where Arthur was taken at the end of his reign to rest. In many Celtic legends, you could enter the otherworld if you were bearing the silver bough of apples. In Celtic mythology, the magical golden apples of the sun had properties of healing and immortality. An Irish king from the third century named Cormac mac Art had a silver branch with three golden apples. When shaken, the branch made beautiful and magical music that healed the sick and wounded and had the power to lull people to sleep.

Field Guide

The European crab apple (*Malus sylvestris*) tree's descendants are found in many varieties all over the world. All of these apple hybrids go back to the native crab apple indigenous to the British Isles. Apple trees are believed to be the oldest trees cultivated and are actually a distant relative of the rose. The crab apple is a relatively small tree that is usually less than thirty feet tall. Its bark is brown and rough, and some even retain their thorns from ancient times. This deciduous tree has leaves that are rounded at the base and pointed on the end, and they grow alternately arranged. The crab apple is much smaller than the varieties found in the grocery stores and is sour but good for baking or preserves. Crab apple blossoms have five petals and are a deep rosy shade, while their modern counterparts are very light pink or nearly white. They are covered in delicate blossoms in March–May depending on variety and climate, and they bud leaves and blossoms simultaneously.

Apple trees are self-incompatible and need to cross-pollinate with other trees. Insects such as butterflies and bees pollinate them in the spring. Apple trees bear their ripe, delicious fruit in the fall and are a favorite for Mabon gatherings. All varieties of apples have five carpels (little holes) arranged in a five-pointed star, and each carpel has one to three seeds in it. Wild apple trees originally were spread by their seeds, which would have been deposited by way of animal droppings, and later were planted by humans. Most modern apple trees are propagated asexually by grafting. Some gardeners enjoy cultivating some of the antique varieties of apple trees, as they are a beautiful and important part of our history and culture.

Muin • Vine

Celtic Name: Muin (pronounced *muhn*), "back"

Letter: M

Status: Chieftain

Divining Charm

> *The strongest of effort has been your course*
> *The work of the back for a man, ox, or horse*
> *Celebrate your completion as your harvest you share*
> *The highest of beauty with abundance to spare.*

Divinatory Meaning: Completion, harvest

You've worked hard, and your efforts are coming to fruition. Take some time to celebrate and revel in all you have accomplished in life so far. Let go of your inhibitions a bit, and just have a good time. If you're facing a financial struggle, that time is coming to an end; if you remember to count the blessings of what you do have instead of regretting what you don't have, the universe will reward you with more of what you are grateful for. Share some of your blessings, and they'll return to you many times over.

Reversed Meaning

Take care that you aren't allowing yourself to waste your assets or get weighed down by excessive overindulgence. Enjoying life is important, but if it's all you do, then you'll never accomplish your goals. Make sure that your roots are

muin
VINE

strong or you won't be able to climb any higher, and you may lose your footing.

Symbolism and Lore

The muin/vine card depicts the ripening fruit of the vine as it climbs upward. A representation of a Green Man, a Celtic stylized foliate head, is carved into the stone wall. The Green Man is a symbol for prosperity and the growth of the land. We see a ritual sharing of wine in the foreground—the wonderful product of the hard work of growing a vineyard and the long process of fermentation. The wine is in an ancient cup carved out of a single piece of red amber that was found in an ancient Celtic barrow mound site in Hove, England. While thought of as a stone, amber is actually fossilized tree resin, magically tied to our most ancient ancestors and to the sun, growth, and pure energy. The scene reminds us to celebrate our successes with joy while remaining responsible to ourselves and others.

While represented here as grapevine, vine can also include blackberry or mulberry, which produced fruit the Celts used to make alcoholic beverages long before grapes were brought into the region. Wine made from grapes began its introduction to the Celts as a luxury and status symbol, and it eventually rivaled the popular libation of mead, a honey wine that was a staple of Celtic celebrations. Vine is a climbing plant, constantly growing higher, reaching toward the heavens. Many poets and seers throughout history have whetted their divine inspiration with wine. Divine inebriation goes back to the cult of Bacchus, part of the culture of the Romans, who introduced wine to the Celts. It was also written in Celtic legends that strong drink was sometimes used to work warriors up into a frenzy before battle, similar to the Viking berserkers. Imagine a bunch of half-drunk, naked, raging Celts painted blue, waving swords, and bellowing war cries; their enemies would be more than a little nervous. The energy of the vine can help us remove our inhibitions and certainly give reason to celebrate.

Field Guide

The common grapevine (*Vitis vinifera*) usually enjoys a warm climate, and although native to the Mediterranean, it was successfully introduced and cultivated in southern Britain during the Bronze Age. There is a large variety of grapes that are grown on every continent except Antarctica.

If left in the wild to climb a tall tree or other support, a grapevine can grow up to a hundred feet tall but usually won't produce much fruit, as all its energy will go into growing. Most vineyards keep grapes pruned to encourage fruiting. Grapevines have flaky, brown bark with many curling tendrils coming off of the main branches. The leaves are alternate and lobed. The growth cycle of the grapevine varies depending upon the weather of the region. In the spring, green buds break out from the old vines that have turned brown over the winter. Leaves will begin to grow, and tiny flowers emerge shortly after. *Vinifera* flowers are hermaphroditic and self-pollinating. Each tiny flower that gets fertilized will quickly begin to grow into a berry, or grape, containing seeds, which will ripen in the fall. The leaves turn a lovely yellow, and the plant moves into dormancy in the winter. Seedless varieties of grapes have been developed to please consumers, and many different varieties of grapes are grown for different wines, but they are all members of the same family, with a rich heritage.

In addition to the grapes that we consume as fruit, wine, juice, and raisins, the rest of the plant is used. The leaves are edible and are rolled into appetizers filled with grains and meat. Grapevines are formed into wreathes, baskets, and other popular decorations.

gort
IVY

Gorт • Ivy

Celtic Name: Gort (pronounced *gort*), "field"

Letter: G

Status: Chieftain

Divining Charm

Sweeter than grass, as the ivy grows wise
Though her stature seems small, see a warrior rise
Tenacious and tough, sweet but never demure
Pleasing to the eye, but survival's assured.

Divinatory Meaning: Tenacity, self

Your survival instinct is strong, even if life has provided tough barriers that seem insurmountable. You have everything you need to rise above and power through whatever is before you. You may not have been given the smooth road; perhaps a rocky path is yours instead. Do not despair, for you can grow and flourish in life situations where others might be defeated. Your path is one of self-discovery, and your life force is strong enough to achieve whatever goals you have set for yourself. Use what is inside of you—the gifts you inherited from your ancestors—and apply them without fear.

Reversed Meaning

You are facing difficulties, and you may feel strangled or restricted. Search inside yourself for the answers—is there an outside force that has you in a stranglehold, or is it your own obstinacy that is holding you back? Also, when ivy appears reversed, watch out for jealousy directed at you.

Symbolism and Lore

Ivy has connections to many of the trees of the ogham and is often found in the wild literally connected to trees. Ivy is a very opportunistic plant that grows on other plants and can even grow on stone. Although at first glance ivy is a seemingly small and charming plant, it can actually harm the mightiest trees of the forest with its relentless grip, so it is not to be underestimated. This would be why the Celts named it a chieftain tree; they respected the fact that it was tough and able to meet any challenge with grace and beauty. No matter the terrain, ivy will find a way to survive.

In this card, ivy is represented as a beautiful, emerald-eyed forest spirit, clad in green and draped in ivy. She presents the viewer with a bough of ivy, offering you persistence and the power of belief in your own inner strength to carry you through. Her expression portrays self-assurance and depth. There is a suggestion of faerie wings at her shoulders, pointing to the ivy's connection with the good people of the land.

Interestingly, according to folklore, ivy covering your wall will protect the people in the home from dark magic, possibly because the ivy is tougher than any curse. It is believed to be a lucky talisman, especially for women. Ivy was used in love magic to allow a woman to see her future husband. The early Greeks included ivy in bridal bouquets to symbolize fidelity and unending love. Traditional Celtic wedding bouquets combined ivy with thistle and heather. Added to ivy, thistle would have granted the bride protection and heather would signify a loving partnership.

Ivy is associated with holly, as related in the Old English song "The Contest of the Holly and the Ivy," which was later rewritten as a Christmas carol, but the original lyrics paint the picture of a battle of the sexes, using holly and ivy as emblems of man and woman. The two can also be considered a representation of the God and Goddess of the natural world, both evergreen and flourishing in seasons of growth or decline, reminding us that life always continues. The growth of ivy can be seen to duplicate the sacred spiral. This is a pattern that runs throughout all life as DNA, the building blocks of life. Remembering this, ivy can help you bring forth the gifts that your ancestors have given you. Ivy reminds us of tenacity and self, and our genes that have come to us through the ages, against many odds, to make us who we are today.

Field Guide

The English ivy (*Hedra helix*) is native to Europe, was introduced into North America by settlers, and is commonly planted as an ornamental plant. Ivy is an evergreen vine with dark green leaves that are waxy, with palmate veins. The shape of the leaves varies but is usually a three- to five-lobed leaf with a heart-shaped base. Ivy is very invasive and will trail along the ground and also climb up trees, trellises, stone walls, and brick buildings, usually damaging the surface of the structures it grows on by digging in its strong tendrils, which can even break rock and mortar.

Ivy can grow eighty to one hundred feet long in both sun and shade. Ivy that grows in sunlight produces clusters of greenish-yellow flowers that mature into black, fleshy berries in late fall. Many birds feed on the berries, which are toxic to humans, and spread the seeds, allowing the plant to take over forested regions if planted in rural areas. Ivy is very beautiful, and in addition to being used in gardens for landscaping, it is also a lovely addition to indoor planters due to its tolerance for shade. It is often seen in flower arrangements.

Ngetal • Broom or Reed

Celtic Name: Ngetal (pronounced *NYEH-tl*), "wound"

Letter: NG

Status: Shrub

Divining Charm

The physician's strengths include herbs one and all
With compassion and knowledge may your illness fall
While sweeping away darkness from body and soul
In the physician's robe, heroic deeds make you whole.

Divinatory Meaning: Cleansing, vitality

A remedy for your difficulties is at hand. If you are ill at ease, you must take action, first clearing away physical and emotional toxins in order to protect your vitality. In order to heal the body, take a holistic approach, healing mind, body, and spirit together. You may be someone whose purpose is to bring healing to others; either way, remember any wise healer, whether mainstream physician or spiritual healer, always tempers healing with common sense. Shelter the spirit with the power of hearth and home, and allow harmony to shelter the body and mind.

Reversed Meaning

You may have accumulated negativity, either from outside forces or from within, that must be removed in order for you to be healthy. You have a need for the physical cleansing of

ngetal
BROOM OR REED

your environment and your life. There are lingering issues that need to be swept away—they are drawing away your life force and blocking your road to health and wellness. In addition, take stock of your health—a physical checkup couldn't hurt.

Symbolism and Lore

You will notice that there are two plants associated with the NG/ngetal ogham, broom and reed. While neither would be considered a traditional tree, both are part of the tree ogham and an important part of Celtic society. There are actually several versions of some of the ogham definitions; I have chosen to use both in this card, finding that the plants work in tandem for the meaning. The poetic ogham references all refer to broom and healing, but some texts point to reed and taking action and also balance and harmony. Both of these plants were associated with the home.

In the ngetal/broom or reed card, we see the village medicine woman outside of her Celtic roundhouse. Herbs used for healing hang drying below the roof of her cozy shelter, thatched with the reed that grows nearby. Broom grows in the field beyond, and she sweeps away spiritual negativity and physical refuse with the swoosh of the besom she has skillfully fashioned from broom stems. She keeps her house, which is also where she treats the complaints of the village, in good order. It is clean, safe, and hospitable, a good environment for the work of a healer.

Both broom and reed were used for thatching roofs, for weaving baskets and mats, and for sweeping the home clean, which is essential to preserve health and vitality. These uses associate both plants with hearth and home, warm protection, and wellness. These were the plants used to keep the rain and cold out of the homes, to carry food and medicinal herbs and preparations, and to keep the home environment clean and habitable. In a pinch, reed tubers could be eaten for nourishment, and broom was employed in many medicinal preparations.

Field Guide

Broom (*Cytisus scoparius*) is a native plant to England and is found all over Europe, Asia, and North America. An evergreen, broom is found growing on sandy heaths and pastures, and reaches a height of three to five feet, consisting of many straight, thin green branches with very few tiny oblong leaflets. It produces large, fragrant yellow blooms from April to July that are pollinated by bees. The flowers actually expel large amounts of pollen onto bees when they land on them. Once pollinated, broom produces dark brown 1½-inch seed pods. When mature, they actually burst with a crack, flinging seeds about. After the seed pods burst, the harvest of broom could begin, as it was considered bad luck to use broom for domestic use while it was still in bloom.

Phragmites australis is a reed that is common all over the world. It is considered a grass, and it grows in large stands in marshy regions and along river banks. Reed grows to at least six feet tall but can get up to nineteen feet tall during a hot summer under ideal growing conditions. Its leaves are very long and thin, and are nearly as tall as the plant itself.

It reproduces both sexually and asexually, both by seeds and rhizomes. In late summer, it produces full, dark purplish, feathery flower heads, which, when harvested, can be used for thatching or bundled into brooms called *walis*. Its seed production seems to be used mainly for starting a new reed bed; once a reed bed has been established, it usually spreads quickly through shoots that are part of the root system. There are areas in the British Isles that use reed for thatched roofs to this day.

straif
BLACKTHORN

Scraif · Blackthorn

Celtic Name: Straif (pronounced *strahf*), "sulphur"

Letter: ST

Status: Chieftain

Divining Charm

> *Though with careful effort you may embark*
> *A challenger's arrow still can make its mark*
> *You cannot avoid the red stain of the sword*
> *As secrets increase, strife will not be ignored.*

Divinatory Meaning: Adversity, sacrifice

Sometimes, no matter how hard you try to avoid trouble, it finds you anyway; this is the natural order. You are facing a wound, either physical or emotional, and it is a completely unavoidable situation. This loss may be connected to your being in the service of another, but even injury from a noble act of self-sacrifice is painful. You may be dealing with a backstabber. In this inevitable situation, your focus should be on doing damage control after the fact, and then healing. This is the harsh reality of life; just get through this obstacle. Once you have reached it, it cannot be undone, only dealt with.

Reversed Meaning

You are facing a direct threat to the order in your life. There are secrets—things that are hidden from you, enemies hidden in the mist that want to bring harm. Blackthorn may also warn of an accidental physical injury or impending surgery.

Symbolism and Lore

Shillelagh in hand, a man walks along the blackthorn hedges. Strolling along, minding his own business, he feels a sharp pain and a curse escapes his lips as if something has bitten him. He reaches for the wound, realizing that the long, sharp barb of the blackthorn has snagged his arm, drawing both blood and sharp pain; his shillelagh is no defense this time. The sting of the blackthorn is terrible, but what's done is done. He will have to make an unexpected detour to see the village healer, for he knows an injury from a blackthorn can easily become angry with infection if left untreated.

Knotted and twisted, the dark wood of the blackthorn looks ancient and brings to mind an older time when shillelaghs were the national weapon of rural Ireland. Some even hollowed out the "hitting" end and filled it with molten lead for more weight. The Irish used this one- or two-foot-long stick of hard, knobby blackthorn as a weapon so dangerous that shillelaghs were outlawed during the last English occupation in the early 1900s. Undaunted, the Irishmen just made them longer; it would have seemed improper to outlaw a man's walking stick. The appeal of the classic blackthorn walking stick is probably equal parts beauty, Old World appeal, and rebellion!

Blackthorn was often used for hedges—to divide property and to keep both people and livestock where they were supposed to be. It grows in thick, and its long, sharp thorns make it an impenetrable barrier. A hedge is a mystical symbol of the place between the physical and the astral realms. Interestingly, blackthorn blossoms are considered a symbol of both life and death at the same time, because the blackthorn blossoms while there are no leaves on the plant, only blossoms and thorns.

Bringing blackthorn blossoms into your home or wearing them is extremely bad luck. The ashes of blackthorn wreathes, however, bring good luck to the wheat fields in some rural areas in England to this day. The Irish believed that a specific variety of faeries called the Lunatishees were the guardians of blackthorns. The Lunatishees forbid the cutting of blackthorn branches before November 11 or after May 11, their sacred days. Mortals who are foolish enough to ignore this rule may meet with horrible misfortune.

Field Guide

The blackthorn (*Prunus spinosa*) is native to Europe, Asia, and northwest Africa, and it is also found sporadically in parts of the United States. It's a deciduous plant that only grows to about fifteen feet tall, although it is often pruned into a shorter hedge. Blackthorn likes sandy soil and also is happy growing in soil where there is lots of limestone and humus. It tends to have irregularly shaped branches that are covered with black bark and very sharp, long thorns. The flowers are creamy white, with five petals; they are hermaphroditic and pollinated by insects. The blackthorn bursts into bloom during cold snaps early in the spring, in February or March, shortly before the leaves come in. These cold snaps are sometimes called "blackthorn winters." The white blooms against the otherwise bare black, twisted branches look quite striking.

The leaves come out after the petals fall and are oval and serrated. They have a down to them when they are young but become smooth as they mature. The pollinated flowers form fruit with a single stonelike seed that ripens in the fall, called a sloe. They are waxy and black, with a blue-purple cast. Sloes are harvested in late October through early November, usually after the first frost. Animals eat the sloes, dispersing the seeds, which is how blackthorn propagates. Sloes are used to make preserves, syrups, and a liqueur called sloe gin. The blossoms are edible, and the leaves have been used to make tea. The wood of the blackthorn is very hard and knotty, but since it doesn't get very big, the best use for the wood is walking sticks, which are highly prized.

Ruis • Elder

Celtic Name: Ruis (pronounced *rweesh*), "reddening"

Letter: R

Status: Shrub

Divining Charm

A face is blushing and reddening from shame
Someone was wronged and someone is blamed
The glow of anger may bring a downfall
Retribution shall come as sure as nightfall.

Divinatory Meaning: Consequence, regret

You or someone else may be feeling regret over a deed that isn't a proud one. A situation may have caused you embarrassment or didn't work out the way you planned. If you wronged someone else or were wronged yourself, karma may be circling around to take care of the matter. Remember, if you have made an unwise choice that harmed someone else, you can only take responsibility for it, make atonement, and then learn so you don't make similar errors in the future. Once you have made things right, holding on to regret is a waste of precious energy. If someone wronged you, one way or another, he or she needs to be confronted, allowing him or her an opportunity to be forgiven and you to heal. Elder can also herald a new residence, a new career, or health changes, all situations of moving on.

ruis
ELDER

Reversed Meaning

There is a situation dealing with humiliation that needs to be resolved. There may be a vendetta in motion—someone seeking revenge. Revenge is in the air; someone will face the consequences of their actions, and no one escapes from themselves.

Symbolism and Lore

The ruis/elder card portrays the goddess Macha. She married a mortal farmer in secret and told him as long as he didn't tell anyone his wife was a goddess, she would stay with him. She became pregnant with twins, and in her last month, her husband went off to an assembly. There were many competitions there, one being a horse race. Her husband began to brag that his wife could beat any horse in the race, even the king's horse. Macha was dragged to the fair by the Ulster men despite her pleading that she was about to give birth. No one would help her, and she was forced to race the king's horse while in labor to prevent her husband from being killed for his bragging and insult to the king. Furious, she ran the race and won, and then proceeded to give birth to her twins before the stunned men, who probably realized at this point their error in judgment. She then placed a curse upon the Ulster men that in their time of crisis, they would experience her labor pains. The men were unable to fight during the Cattle Raid of Cooley, and the hero Cuchulainn had to fight by himself while the men were all in labor for days.

Elder is associated with the goddess figure of the Elder Mother and has long been connected with witches and magic.

The trees were also known to exact retribution of their own. Woodsmen had a traditional charm that was spoken respectfully if they took wood from an elder tree to prevent bad luck from coming to them: "Lady Ellhorn, give me some of thy wood, and I will give thee some of mine when it grows in the forest." Wood taken can be fashioned into talismans for good luck or protection, but to burn elder wood is extremely bad luck. There is a legend that tells of a witch who confronted the Danish king and his entourage while they were trying to invade England. Chanting magical words, she tricked him and turned him and his men into the famous Rollright Stones before transforming herself into an elder tree.

Field Guide

Black elder (*Sambucus nigra*) is a native plant of Europe. There are many regional varieties that can be found all over the world. In the United States, we find American elder (not to be confused with box elder, which isn't actually an elder but is in the maple family). Elders can grow in a variety of conditions but do love the sun.

The elder is deciduous and doesn't grow very tall—ten to eighteen feet is average. Its bark is light gray when young but darkens and becomes rough with age. Its leaves are opposite pairs, usually between five and seven leaflets, occasionally nine. The leaves come out in the spring. In midsummer, elderflowers bloom in large white clusters. Each flower has five petals, is hermaphroditic, and is pollinated mostly by flies. In autumn, the fruit of the elder tree becomes ripe and full. Elderberries are dark purple, almost black, and grow in large clusters on purplish stalks that droop from their weight. They are eaten by birds that spread the seeds around the countryside.

Elderberry wine is made of both elderberries and flowers. Elderberries are used for making jams, pies, and preserves. It would be unwise to eat elderberries unless you know what you're doing, as they are mildly poisonous when not fully ripe.

ailim
SILVERFIR OR ELM

Ailim • Silverfir or Elm

Celtic Name: Ailim (pronounced *AHLm*), "elm"

Letter: A

Status: Shrub

Divining Charm

A grand perspective brings into sight
The loudest of groanings in darkness or light
You may marvel at wonders and take in the view
The beginning of answers they bring to you.

Divinatory Meaning: Delight, awe

You are very aware of life and your place in it. You find yourself in amazement as patterns unfold around you, having reached a new perspective that allows you to see the bigger picture. Although coming to a realization may sometimes cause you pain, your awareness of a situation can ultimately work to your advantage. It's important to express your emotions right now. Don't hold back, whether it's in joy, sorrow, or anger; own your feelings and speak your peace. You have come to a position of strength. New opportunities are opening before you; don't fear them, but use them well.

Reversed Meaning

You may have allowed yourself to be overcome by fear. Worry and fear can lead you to a point of inaction. Instead of keeping calm, you are giving in to confusion. Your best course of action is to seek out a new vantage point and work out your emotional issues, express your feelings, and release them so you can move forward.

Symbolism and Lore

Although the ogham letter ailim is often associated with the fir tree, it is also associated with the elm, which is what the word *ailim* translates to. The ailim card portrays both trees growing next to each other. Two sisters have climbed this pair of grand trees side by side. It was a challenge for the two young girls, sometimes scary, but they went on, talking, laughing, and sometimes crying out when a foot slipped, climbing steadily until they reached the top. Looking out over the countryside, a gasp escapes their lips at the amazing sight; the view takes their breath away. It is scary up there in the treetops—the wind blowing, branches creaking—but exhilarating too. Now that they have this new vantage point, they know that it's not only a beautiful sight but a clear map of where they've been and where they're going. They can see the best path to their destination.

Fir trees have long been associated with life and immortality because they are evergreens. Evergreens were brought in the house during winter festivals as a reminder of life that survives through the cold season of winter. Later, they were adapted as a Yule or Christmas tree, the soft needles of the fir being a popular choice. Fir needles were burned to magically ease childbirth, symbolizing the Mother Goddess in her eternal vigor.

Elm trees are a symbol of hope coming to fruition, a quality also associated with the vine, as it was once used for training grape vines on when the Romans first introduced them. There was a Celtic tribe called the Lemovices who lived in the Gallic regions; their name means "people of the elm." The elm has been used magically for comfort, protection, wisdom, and eloquence in speaking.

Field Guide

Silverfir (*Abies alba*) is a tree that is native to mountain habitats all over Europe. It grows between 130 and 165 feet tall, and it is a coniferous evergreen. Its has flattened, flexible needles that are dark green on top, with two pale green stripes along the bottom. The needles have a small notch in the tip. The silverfir's bark is gray and smooth, with resin blisters, becoming scaly with age. In the spring, it produces small brown pollen cones bearing two-winged seeds that are pollinated by the wind when they mature in the autumn.

Its resin has been long used to make varnishes and pitch for sealing wooden vessels. Fir trees produce a soft wood harvested for holiday trees, general construction, and paper manufacture.

English elm (*Ulmus procera*) was once one of the tallest and fastest-growing deciduous trees in Europe and is believed to have been introduced by the Romans. Dutch elm disease, a fungus, wiped out many elms both in Europe and in America. The elm enjoys full sun, often growing to over 130 feet tall. Its leaves are simple, toothed, almost oval, alternately attached, and a dark shade of green. The elm produces hermaphroditic flowers with reddish-purple flowers in February and March, before the leaves emerge. They are pollinated by the wind, producing clusters of round, winged seeds, the majority of which are not viable, so the elm is mostly propagated by shoots. The elm is mostly used in modern times as an ornamental tree but is still used to grow grapevines on in some areas.

Ohn • Gorse

Celtic Name: Ohn (pronounced *uhn*), "gorse"

Letter: O

Status: Chieftain

Divining Charm

The strength of a warrior's passions abound
Or the gentlest of work and the heart it shall pound
Whether fierceness in battle or passion for love
Your strength of the heart you are not bereft of.

Divinatory Meaning: Passion, strength

The strength and passion of a warrior and that of a lover are not actually that different; after all, the saying goes that all is fair in love and war. This card represents the dichotomy of both. We may be spiritual beings, but we live in the material realm, and you may be feeling the need to express that in physical ways. Celebrate your being; your life force and vitality are high, and combining forces with another can bring great rewards. Don't give up; express your lust for life. There may be a passionate and physical love affair that features prominently. The promise of a bright, warm future and rewards for hard work are assured.

Reversed Meaning

If you get too wrapped up in your passion, you may forget to watch out for the thorns! Are you having a good time, or

ohn
GORSE

are you taking too many risks and endangering your heart or your well-being? You may be heading toward a sticky entanglement that you would do best to avoid.

Symbolism and Lore

A young couple of warriors are sparring amongst the blooming gorse in the warm sun. Oblivious to the couple, bees work steadily toward their own goals. What started off as a playful training session soon escalates into a passionate battle, each feeling like they have something to prove to the other—their skill, talent, and strength are all under scrutiny by their partner. In the heat of the battle, amongst the fragrance of the gorse flowers, a moment passed into being that changed everything; their skills evenly matched, the strength of battle changed into other passions evenly matched as well. Their eyes lock, and something that had been brewing in both of them comes to fruition. The success of a people depends upon their ability to protect and defend as well as to love.

Gorse, sometimes called furze, is a fascinating plant that grows in a mass of deep yellow blooms. It is strongly scented and has been compared with coconut and vanilla; it is said that when gorse is in bloom, it is the season for kissing. Gorse blooms almost continuously, so there is always time for love! This also secured gorse's place as a symbol of fertility. Gorse attracts many bees and is a symbol of achievement through hard work, as well as a signifier of honey production, which means there will be honey for making mead. Gorse was very important to the Celts, especially the heath dwellers, who used it as fuel for fires when trees were scarce. Gorse was also the best laundry line around; its spiny thorns didn't let the clothes blow away, and the blooms left the clothing smelling fresh. In the early spring, farmers often burn fields of gorse to clear the woody stems and spines, encouraging new soft, green growth that cattle and sheep love to feed on. The yellow blossoms covering the hillsides are also associated with the sun and often with Lugh, the sun god, further adding to its associations with fertility, creative energy, and vitality. Gorse is also known as a protective plant against dark magic or curses, protecting happiness and well-being.

Field Guide

Common gorse (*Ulex europeaeus*) is native to Europe, although it has many close relatives found in Europe and parts of Africa and Iberia. Gorse is found in the United States, where it was introduced as an ornamental plant in the middle to late 1800s and is now considered an invasive species due to its aggressive nature.

Gorse thrives in sunny, sandy areas and grows in abundance on the heaths. It grows to around eight to sixteen feet tall. When left to grow, its stems can become woody and light colored, with a yellowish-green tint. Its bark is thin and flaky. Young leaves are thin and divided into three leaflets growing off a main stem; as the plant ages, its leaves become small spines. Its tender shoots also become modified into spines. Gorse has a very long blooming season, while the height of its blooms occurs in spring. Its flowers are lipped and are pollinated by bees. Once pollinated, a seed pod forms, which loudly pops open in the heat of the sun or by the disturbance of passing bees and livestock, shooting its seeds out. If this sounds familiar, you are correct: gorse is a cousin of broom.

Gorse is still used as cattle fodder; in addition, its flowers are edible and are used in salads, as well as for making gorse flower wine.

ur
HEATHER

Ur · Heather

Celtic Name: Ur (pronounced *oor*), "earth"

Letter: U

Status: Shrub

Divining Charm

Take in the scent of the good green earth
Your clan is complete and joined in mirth
A partnership grows from beginning to end
Transforming the old and progressing again.

Divinatory Meaning: Transition, partnership

The energies of the past have been cast into the cauldron and are reborn as a powerful and nurturing partnership. This relationship may tell of romance or business collaboration. This is a down-to-earth relationship that has allowed you to cast away the past and start over fresh and new. If you are already involved, you are possibly moving into a new stage of your feelings for each other or further securing that connection. There is a sense of confidence that is of mutual benefit to both parties. You have a good foundation, which will allow both to grow as this kinship transitions to the next level. Keep your roots firm but allow yourself and your partner space to grow and branch out, and great things will blossom. The future is wide open.

Reversed Meaning

A partnership may be moving faster than you feel comfortable with; perhaps there needs to be a stronger foundation before moving on. You or the other person may be expecting more than the other can return, and this may lead to conflicts. Take a step back and allow things to progress naturally, without trying to direct everything too much; take it day by day.

Symbolism and Lore

We see a couple of the heath upon a small mound, joined in a handfasting ceremony, which was a very old marriage rite where the couple's hands were tied together to symbolize their union. The heather is blooming all across the countryside, and from this vantage point we can see off into the distance toward the horizon and the sun that shines down upon all the land. Beneath their joined hands is an ornate silver cauldron filled with heather blooms. This cauldron is symbolic of the transition from the past into the future and has also long been a symbol of abundance and rebirth. Many vessels and artifacts from the time have been retrieved from peat bogs all over the Celtic lands. This one bears a striking resemblance to the famous Gundestrup cauldron.

Heather is a plant of the heath, and many legends abound of the good Celtic people finding a makeshift bed in fields of soft, welcoming heather. It was also tied together to make mattresses in the home that were reportedly very comfortable as well as having a restorative scent. Heather branches were also sometimes used for thatching and brooms in some areas, and were even used for firewood, adding to its attributes of well-being and security.

Most heather flowers are purple, but occasionally you'll find a small patch of white heather. White heather is considered very good luck and is sometimes used in Scottish wedding bouquets. It was also considered a good amulet for protection. There is speculation that the very word *heathen* was taken from the same root as the word for *heather*, being the people and the plant of the heath.

The Scottish people have made a wonderful libation called heather ale for centuries. A legend says that a Pictish king fought to the death rather than reveal his people's recipe for the drink they were so well known for. Heather ale is produced commercially today but is hard to find; if you enjoy sampling specialty and microbrewery beers, I highly recommend it.

Field Guide

Common heather (*Calluna vulgaris*) is a native plant to many parts of Europe, including the British Isles as well as areas in Spain, Russia, Scandinavia, Turkey, and Morocco. It has been introduced in parts of North America. It became an invasive species when introduced to Australia and New Zealand. Heather likes to grow in a wide range of climates and doesn't mind acidic soils; it is most often found on hillsides, moors, and heaths.

Heather is a small, bushy evergreen that grows up to around twenty-four inches tall on average but can reach up to almost four feet tall. A heather shrub can live for over thirty years. Its leaves are dark green and scalelike, curling in at the edges. Its branches are dark brown. Heather begins to flower in July, and the peak of its flowering season is in August. Its purplish-pink blossoms are abundant; the flowers are very small and bell-shaped, with four petals, and are pollinated mostly by insects, especially bees, who make prized heather honey. The petals turn into brown capsules holding up to thirty seeds, which are dispersed either by wind or passing animals that knock the seed pods as they pass by. Heather can also reproduce by shoots, making it a very prolific plant.

eadha · aspen

Celtic Name: Eadha (pronounced *EH-yah*), "aspen"

Letter: E

Status: Shrub

Divining Charm

Aspen, the fair birch's kinsman, may tremble
But right by your side as you test your mettle
It's distinguished and brave going into the fight
A true friend in battle to rally your might.

Divinatory Meaning: Courage, steadfastness

You are in a position where you will have an opportunity to face and to conquer your fear. You will see a way to use your feelings of apprehension as a friend. You will find courage within you for the battle ahead, and you will be steadfast in your decisions. You will find great strength as you battle your own dark side, and you will need those lessons in order to progress as you embrace your warrior spirit. You will undergo a test of your mettle. Remember, when a person has courage, it doesn't mean that they are never afraid; it means that they are able to overcome that fear in order to do what simply must be done. Sometimes the right thing to do isn't the easy thing.

eadha
ASPEN

Reversed Meaning

You are allowing your fears to get the better of you. Your anxiety over a problem or series of problems has you at a standstill, unable to act. You must look your fear in the eye, allow it to pass over you, and come to the realization that you are more powerful than the worries that you face. Only then can you become the warrior that you need to be in order to face this test.

Symbolism and Lore

The eadha/aspen card shows an overhead view of distinguished aspen trees towering toward the sky. A warrior woman has summoned her inner strength and charges forward to battle. She is reminiscent of Scathach, who was the master warrior that gave the Irish hero Cuchulainn his training. Scathach would have gained her mastery of the warrior's arts by preparing herself properly in mind, body, and spirit and learning to overcome the fear that can leave one unable to act when necessary. She is also associated with the Isle of Skye, where aspen trees used to grow heavily and where some still remain to this day. In the card, the aspen leaves tremble around the warrior in the light breeze; a few have fallen from their branches. She knows that her time for trembling has passed. Inspired by the aspens around her, she draws up the strength of her shadow side in the form of a fierce war cry and goes bravely forward with her leather-covered aspen shield.

One of the magical lessons that the aspen has for us is to keep our roots strong and to draw upon our connection to others for strength in times of need. This tree has long been a "test tree" and associated with conquering fear due to the fact that its leaves tremble in the lightest of breezes, but the tree remains strong.

The society of the Celts was a warrior society where men and women fought side by side. That place between fear and courage would have been a mystical place of decision, of the unseen world. The aspen appears right before the yew in the ogham alphabet, which represents a gateway of mortality. These two associations show that one must embrace both life and the concept of death in order to find the strength to face a test or a battle.

Field Guide

The aspen (*Populus tremula*) is the smallest member of the poplar family. This deciduous tree can grow up to sixty-five feet in height, in comparison with its other poplar cousins that can grow to a hundred feet. Aspen is a native tree to the British Isles and is linked to ancient woodlands found in Scotland. Aspens are found in many areas all over Europe and the United States, famously in the Rocky Mountains. In the spring, some trees bear light-colored male catkins, while others bear greenish female catkins that seed in May. Aspen trees reproduce more often by suckering than by fertilization and tend to grow in large colonies. All the trees interconnected by the roots in this way are called clones. They all bud and blossom at the same time in the spring and turn exactly the same golden shade in the fall.

The aspen's trunk remains very thin for its height, and its silvery-gray bark is covered with black diamond shapes. Its leaves are rounded and grow on alternate sides of the stem with a very long, flattened stalk, and they turn a golden yellow in the fall. Individual aspen trees can live from 40 to 150 years, with the oldest individual aspen tree, or "stem," ever recorded at 320 years old. The root systems, or "clones," of the aspen are much longer-lived than the aspen trees themselves. A stand of aspen is really one huge organism in which the main source of life is a system of roots underground, and each tree grows from that same vast root system, with trees springing up and dying over the years while the root system remains. The oldest known of these systems in existence, called Pando and known as "the trembling giant," covers 106 acres and is located in Bryce Canyon National Park in central Utah. It is considered to be one organism and is believed to be an astounding eighty thousand years old; it has been nominated as the largest living organism in the world.

idho
YEW

Idho • Yew

Celtic Name: Idho (pronounced *EE-yoh*), "yew"

Letter: I

Status: Peasant

Divining Charm

The oldest of woods has come into view
The crone at your service, she summons to you
Now you know a rite of passage does await
Leave something behind as you step through the gate.

Divinatory Meaning: Gateway, mortality

One aspect of life is diminishing; you are facing a big change, a transformational period. Something is coming to an end, but something new will replace it. You are giving up an aspect of yourself to become reinvented—it may be a promotion, a career change, a breakup, or even a marriage. The yew indicates death, but probably only a symbolic one; consider this a rite of passage as you leave something behind. You will also embrace something new, so face it without fear, knowing that change for good or bad is difficult, but you will grow from it. Everything that begins has an end at some point too; it's all part of life. Yew is also a tree of immortality, reminding us that energy doesn't disappear, it merely transforms.

Reversed Meaning

You face a difficult change—possibly a loss or a very serious reminder that nothing in life is forever—and you are likely to lament this situation. You'll need to try to find acceptance and move toward release. A death, even a symbolic one, reminds us of our place in the world and to treasure all of our blessings.

Symbolism and Lore

A giant, lone yew tree has stood for over a thousand years; it has become so old that it has split, leaving an opening, a passageway to the next realm. The crone is there to greet you—she is the loving grandmother and facilitator there to assist you from one life into another. She wears a shift of natural weave as a reminder that she represents the natural progression of the natural world. She stirs the magical cauldron of life, death, and rebirth; this is the mystical place of transformation. You notice a holed stone around her neck; it is an amulet for protection. Although you are stepping into the unknown that lies before you, you feel strangely comforted, knowing that this is all part of the great tapestry.

The yew is the longest-living tree found in the ogham, living for well over a thousand years. It is a very sacred tree, associated with life, death, and rebirth, and also with immortality. Yews were so revered that when Christianity took over the Celtic regions, many of the already ancient yew trees were left standing, and church cemeteries were built around them.

As well as apple and oak, the yew was a wood of choice for a druid's wand, these woods being the wise and knowledgeable purveyors of darkness, light, and the natural mysteries. Yew was also a wood that was prized for making longbows, perhaps further adding to its reputation of being a life-changing force for good or bad—depending on what side of the arrow you were on, of course.

Field Guide

The common yew or European yew (*Taxus baccata*) is an evergreen native to many parts of Europe, northwest Africa, and northern Iran. There are many close relatives of the common yew that are planted as decorative shrubs all over the United States. The European yew grows to be anywhere between thirty and sixty-six feet tall on average when left to grow without pruning. Its trunk can get rather wide, anywhere from around six to thirteen feet in diameter. A yew tree growing this wide tends to hollow with age. They also tend to grow in fluted lobes, making the age potential of the yew tree difficult to pinpoint. According to recent research by dendrochronologists (who analyze tree rings), some of the yew trees found in British church yards may date back as far as four thousand years, making them much older than even the American giant redwoods.

The bark of the yew tree is thin, brown, and scaly, flaking in small sections. The wood is an orange-brown with an interesting grain. It has dark green, flexible needles that are lighter in color on the underside and arranged spirally on green stems. The yew is usually dioecious, producing either male or female cones on one plant, but occasionally it does produce both. A yew tree also occasionally changes sexes. The male cones shed their pollen in early spring and pollinate female cones by wind. In six to nine months, the yew produces a bright red berrylike aril, a fleshy structure containing one seed. These are eaten by birds and dispersed, although the seeds themselves are highly toxic. Most of the yew tree is highly poisonous, and it is recommended that you wear gloves while handling it and never ingest any part of it.

Koad · Grove

Celtic Name: Koad (pronounced *code*), "sacred space"

Letter: CH

Status: None

Divining Charm

The grove is yours by oak, ash, and thorn
For all that has passed and all that is born
Are part of each other, connected as one
As all that is lost and all that is won.

Divinatory Meaning: Oneness, consciousness

Wisdom is readily available to you; you need only to look within. There are connections between events that you may not have seen before, but those connections are very important in helping you to see through the illusions that are at hand. The situation may be more complicated than you realize; try to see the situation as a whole rather than focusing on the individual aspects. Also don't forget that the decisions you make will ripple out to others, so act responsibly and teach others by your example. Things may seem very complex, so be careful not to miss the forest for the trees.

Reversed Meaning

You may be involved in resolving a conflict, which will be difficult because of the complexity of the situation. There is

koad
GROVE

a lot of confusion; try to back up and see the whole picture. Don't get bogged down in the details.

Symbolism and Lore

Taliesin, the famous bard, was a man very much in touch with the concept of oneness. Oneness is a belief that we are not only connected to everything, we are actually part of everything on a very deep level. Previously known as Gwion Bach, Taliesin was reborn of the goddess Cerridwen after a shapeshifting battle of wits and born with the knowledge of everything in the world and his place in it. As an infant he spoke in verse, proclaiming that knowledge. He also spoke that he remembered having been a blue salmon, a dog, a stag, a roebuck on the mountain, a stock, a spade, an axe in the hand, a stallion, a buck, a bull, and a grain of the fields. In this card, Taliesin rejoices in the oneness of the universe and takes his place within the magical, sacred grove of trees.

Groves were the temples of the druids and of many other people of earth-based faiths. A grove is a gathering of trees with a clearing in the center; many of the trees in the druids' sacred groves were the faerie triad of oak, ash, and hawthorn. Apple, willow, beech, and yew were trees often traditionally associated with the sacred grove as well. In fact, there are as many sacred groves as there are forests, all trees being sacred. This was a place where all knowledge came together—a place of peace and justice. A sacred grove would have been a place specifically consecrated as a temple, a place simultaneously of the material world and the spirit world. It was magically protected as a place to worship, to raise and send energy, and to gather for council meetings and other judicial events.

Field Guide

You could probably find most of the trees within this deck as part of a sacred grove. A field guide to help you identify sacred groves is much less scientific and more spiritual than identifying the individual trees within the grove.

So how do you locate a sacred grove? Well, there are many sacred sites to visit in the British Isles and Celtic regions, such as the Fairy Glen at Rosemarkie on the Black Isle or the Druid Oaks of Avalon at Glastonbury. Sadly, when the Romans invaded, they burned most of the druids' groves and ceremonial sites. Of course, the land that the sacred groves once stood on can still be visited. There, under the gentle hand of the Green Man, the offspring of the original trees of the druids' sacred groves may now populate those areas. Some of the groves that were in secret places may still exist.

To find a sacred grove, go into the wild places anywhere in the world and feel with your heart; when you find your grove, you will know. Or better yet, plant one of your own. You could plant an apple orchard or oak, ash, and hawthorn trees in your own yard. I dream of someday having enough land to plant all of the ogham trees that will grow in my region. Remember, sacred space is where you make it, and we actually live within one big grove.

In order to make a spiritual effort to honor the trees, you could also make a donation to a charity that plants trees to help renew the earth. If you visit www.voiceofthetrees.com, you can donate a tree to the Voice of the Trees grove we've dedicated to help replant the Caledonian Forest in Scotland.

oir
SPINDLE

Oir • Spindle

Celtic Name: Oir (pronounced *OO-r*), "spindle"

Letter: TH

Status: Peasant

Divining Charm

Patient work you will need to fulfill
Your knowledge and skill indispensable
Your tasks bring honor to you and your clan
And community spirit be you woman or man.

Divinatory Meaning: Obligation, discipline

You will need self-discipline in order to stay focused and complete your tasks at hand. The work that you do is very important and honorable; you can take pride in your accomplishments. Your skills are needed by your family and perhaps even by your community, and your abilities have the potential to boost your status. You may be up for a promotion, more responsibility, or even a new career. A new opportunity may come as a big surprise or a sudden change, as the wheels seem to have been set in motion by outside forces. Your ability to make something out of nothing may benefit you as you attempt to roll with these changes in an unselfish manner.

Reversed Meaning

Patience is your focus at this time; the winds of change are blowing, but you must allow things to happen in their own time. Meet your current obligations before moving forward with other activities. Take this time to spin your own thread and plan while you wait for the outside forces that weave the future.

Symbolism and Lore

A spindle tree is seen beyond the door of the roundhouse where a woman spins wool into heavy thread. The first spinning wheels weren't what we think of today, with their big wheel and spokes, but were instead simple, rustic drop spindles. The spindle tree's wood is perfect for making a drop spindle because it is very straight, hard wood. This is patient work, but each family and the entire community relied on this important work to clothe them, and the Celts were known for their bright-colored clothing with intricate checks and tartan fabrics. If a woman was skilled and dedicated, she could spin and weave enough for her family and to trade with others, bringing her high status in the clan. The whorl stone on her drop spindle is similar to ones found in archeological digs from the third to fifth centuries. We also see a loom in the background, which she will use to weave her cloth.

Spindle was indeed the wood used to craft its namesake textile tool. In fact, there were even whorl stones found up until the eighth century with ogham and Latin inscriptions carved on them with complimentary messages or blessings on its owner. One can imagine the power of that blessing as the spindle spun away, sending that blessing into the air with every spin, and into each thread as well. Maybe this old practice is why, in the language of flowers, the flowers of the spindle tree mean "your charms are engraven on my heart."

A spindle is a powerful tool indeed. Through hard work, it transforms one thing into another, seeming to do the impossible. Spindles and, later on, spinning wheels became associated with the Fates, the mystical women who hold sway over life and death itself, further pointing to the spindle tree's equal benefits and dangers, as its wood is useful, but its berries are poisonous.

Field Guide

The European spindle (*Euonymus europaeus*), also known as common spindle, is native to most of Europe and can be found as far east as Lithuania, and it is also found in Asia Minor. European spindle has been introduced to the eastern parts of North America, where it is considered an invasive species in some areas. American spindle is also known as burning bush or Eastern wahoo. It's a deciduous shrub that grows between ten and nineteen feet tall. Its bark is smooth and greenish gray with warm brown streaks. It can have single or multiple trunks. Its leaves are simple, oval, very fine-toothed and attached oppositely. Its lime-green flowers have four petals and are hermaphroditic, blossoming in the late spring in small clusters and pollinated by insects.

The fruit of the spindle is pink to reddish purple in color and is an interestingly shaped lobed capsule with four seeds inside. Birds will eat the fruit of the spindle, spreading the seeds, but to most animals and humans it is toxic, possibly resulting in liver and kidney damage or even death.

Most animals won't eat any part of it. The fruit ripens in the autumn and splits open to reveal its seeds. In the autumn, the spindle's leaves turn vibrant shades of orange and reddish purple, hence the nickname of burning bush.

The varieties of spindle are mostly used for ornamental purposes, but its hard wood can be carved to a very fine point and has also been used for violin bows, toothpicks, and charcoal for gunpowder, along with its namesake, textile spindles.

Iphin • Gooseberry

Celtic Name: Iphin (pronounced *IF-in*), "vineyard"

Letter: PE

Status: Peasant

Divining Charm

A mighty success has come to you
Blessings of plenty bring joy anew
Finding good fortune, be it business or pleasure
Your cup is now full, you may drink at your leisure.

Divinatory Meaning: Comfort, success

Success and good fortune are yours in any endeavor. You find comfort in knowing that your needs are met even to the point where you have enough to share with others. You have achieved the status that you have sought after. This card may also represent a person of respect or an important event that will be a good opportunity for you. Prospects are very good through some kind of business transaction, or there may be a contractual agreement or a windfall—perhaps money from the government or a government position. You have every reason to feel self-assured; this card speaks of abundance, status, and joy.

Reversed Meaning

You may be moving away from your comfort zone. While you are anticipating success, you may be allowing fear of that

iphin
GOOSEBERRY

success to prevent abundance from coming your way or staying. Don't continue looking for the bogeyman to bring disappointment. You may have to face challenges to gain your success, but none are so difficult to overcome as your own self-doubt.

Symbolism and Lore

The gooseberry card represents comfort and success. Here, we see a woman of means, probably a clan leader; she is bejeweled, and her high status is obvious. She is dressed in finery of gold and purple. Purple was an expensive dye and hard to come by; she or her husband probably traded for the fabric with a visiting dignitary. She is out relaxing in the sunshine, picking sweet, ripe gooseberries, not because she has to but because she wants to. As she turns, admiring the beauty of the land all around her and secure in her place in it, her bowlful of berries has tipped just a bit, spilling a few, but they won't be missed. She has plenty, and even more are waiting to be picked.

Gooseberry fruit is made into jams, sauces, and pies, and included in stuffing for fowl. Its berries have also been used to make a sweet ale since medieval times. An English favorite is Gooseberry Fool, made by folding cooked gooseberries into sweet, fresh whipped cream. There are gooseberry hedges around many of the ruins in the British Isles; left to grow wild in the countryside, gooseberries were gathered wild long before they were cultivated. Some people call it "currant gooseberry," but while it is in the same family as currants, only true gooseberry has thorns—currants do not—and both plants have different flower and leaf growth. Gooseberry thorns were believed to have the power to rid a person of specific unwanted woes. A folk remedy for a wart was to prick it with a gooseberry thorn passed through a gold wedding ring. It was an old Irish belief that you could get rid of a sty from your eyelid by pointing nine gooseberry thorns at the sty, chanting "away" nine times, and tossing a tenth thorn over your shoulder. Picking gooseberries was an excuse to keep an eye on the young couples who were in need of a chaperone, which is why someone tagging along came to be known as a gooseberry. "Old Gooseberry" is also a nickname for the devil. Dreaming of gooseberries is considered a very fortunate omen.

Field Guide

The European gooseberry (*Ribes grossularia*) is a deciduous shrub native to most of Europe, northwestern Africa, and southwestern Asia. They are in the same family as currants and are closely related to American and pasture gooseberries. The gooseberry usually grows between three and ten feet tall. Its bark is smooth and brown, and the plant sends up new shoots from a large "leg" that grows at ground level. Its leaves are alternate, deeply lobed, and dark green, with small spines at the base of the leaf stalks. In early spring, it produces pink and green bell-shaped flowers laterally along the newer stems.

The flowers are hermaphroditic and are pollinated by wind and insects. The fruit grows singly or doubly and ripens in late summer. European gooseberries are usually around one inch long and are full of tiny seeds. They may be colored bright green, yellow, or shades from pink to very dark purple and are covered in tiny hairs. The fruit is also variegated with light-colored stripes. They are dispersed by the animals that eat the fruit, but they also spread by shoots. Gooseberries are mostly propagated in modern times by cuttings that are planted in autumn, then quickly take root. Gooseberry and blackcurrant hybrids have been produced, and sometimes gooseberry vines are grafted onto currant stalks as well.

uilleand
WOODBINE

Uilleand • Woodbine

Celtic Name: Uilleand (pronounced *ULL-enth*), "woodbine"

Letter: PH

Status: Peasant

Divining Charm

Aware of a great pattern unfolding now
Reveals the truth that was hidden somehow
Stay focused: believe in your own true light
Your true heart's desire, your dreams will take flight.

Divinatory Meaning: Clarity, focus

Secrets will be revealed. There are things that have been hidden, but the way is opening before you—you're in a good position to discover inner knowledge that was veiled before. Your confidence is high, and you may be feeling like you can do anything; of course, if you believe it, you probably can. Patterns previously lost in the shuffle are now coming into view, and the pieces seem to be fitting together like pieces of a puzzle. If you feel you are at the event horizon of discovering the reasons for a situation, look to the heart of the matter. You may notice events trying to attract your attention away from your real goals; you must work to distinguish what's false from what's real. If you can avoid distractions and remain focused, you will find the secrets to your heart's desire at the center of yourself.

Reversed Meaning

You may be faltering in your belief in yourself. You have allowed yourself to become distracted by the wills and intents of others. Put on blinders and stay focused on your goals, and you can reach your most hidden desires.

Symbolism and Lore

On this card, woodbine is shown growing near the entrance of Newgrange ages before it would ever become a famous tourist attraction in Ireland. The entrance stone covered in spirals reminds you that sometimes the way is hidden but energy is swirling all around, and that secret is only temporarily beyond sight. The entrance to the chamber is dark even as the sunlight shines upon the outside, but on the winter solstice, a beam of light from the rising sun is focused right down the passageway, lighting up the chamber in the heart of this mound. A lapwing takes flight; it flies facing you at an angle, flying from the right to the left. In the art of auspicy, this action by a bird foretells of a very good omen.

Woodbine is an old name for the plant commonly known as honeysuckle. In older times, the name honeysuckle was actually applied to meadow clover. Woodbine has also been called fairy trumpets and trumpet flowers. This plant is a favorite of young children, who are naturally drawn to it to pick a pretty blossom, pinch off the base, and sip its sweet nectar. (Okay, I'm a grown woman and still do it occasionally!) It has long been used magically to bring both psychic awareness and prosperity. In addition, woodbine also has a protective quality; if planted near the entrance of a home, it was believed to prevent people with malicious intent from entering, and it guards against hexes and dark magic. A woodbine blossom kept in your purse or wallet is said to prevent it from ever being empty. It was believed that bringing woodbine blossoms indoors would cause lusty dreams for the inhabitants of the home, which is probably why there was a taboo against bringing woodbine into the house during the sexually repressed Victorian era. In the language of flowers, it means "devoted love."

In Scotland, village witches reportedly used woodbine in magical healing rituals, passing the sick patients through a wreath made of woodbine nine times, then cutting it into nine pieces and burning it.

Field Guide

European honeysuckle (*Lonicera periclymenum*), or woodbine, is native to much of Europe, as far north as southern Norway and Sweden, and as far south as North Africa. There are many varieties of honeysuckle that grow all over North America; they have even become an invasive plant in some areas.

Woodbine is a fast-growing, deciduous twining vine that can grow between ten and twenty feet tall on structures like trees, hillsides, or fences. It has tan-colored bark that is smooth when young and becomes rough with age. Its dark green leaves grow early in spring and are simple, opposite, and oval-shaped. Woodbine produces clusters of two-lipped, creamy white flowers with a pinkish-purple tinge. Its flowers are hermaphroditic. Very fragrant during the day, they become even more fragrant at night, being pollinated by butterflies, bees, and moths. Woodbine bears flowers sporadically throughout its growing season, producing clusters of red berries that mature in September. Its leaves drop from the vine green in fall.

Birds eat the berries and spread the seeds, but they are poisonous to humans and most other animals. Woodbine also spreads by shoots and is very easy to transplant and bring attractive insects and hummingbirds to the garden.

phagos · beech

Celtic Name: Phagos (pronounced *FAH-gus*), "beech"

Letter: XI or AE

Status: Chieftain

Divining Charm

Experience has its great lessons to teach
With a teacher or book beneath a fair beech
Taking this opportunity and listening well
You'll learn from the past every story to tell.

Divinatory Meaning: Experience, opportunity

An opportunity is before you to gain from the knowledge of the past. It may come from an old book or the wisdom of someone who has had great life experience. You may even draw upon your own past experiences or those of your family or ancestors. There is a tradition of passing on knowledge, and once it passes from teacher to student, it belongs to the student forever. The lessons of the past can guide you into the future. Revisit the memories of experience in your own life, or listen to the wisdom of a sage or teacher, and be open to guidance. A wise seeker embraces the roles of mentor and of apprentice, learning from both.

Reversed Meaning

Don't neglect lessons of the past, because they have bearing on the present and future; those who don't learn from history

phagos
BEECH

are bound to repeat previous mistakes again and again. Many things that are antiquated still hold value. Don't discount an opportunity to learn from the past.

Symbolism and Lore

A mentor and his young prodigy have met in a beech grove for lessons. Sunlight illuminates them as they sit on a small bluff and work among these great, natural pillars of learning. The mentor is teaching his young student the mysteries of the ogham as he shows him how to carve them upon his staff. The youth will spend many years learning the lessons that each symbol represents at the hand of his patient mentor. The staff will go with him on his travels, reminding him of the knowledge and experience passed on to him.

In the past, beech wood was sometimes used as thin writing tablets and bound together into early books. It is considered one of the best woods for paper pulp. This makes beech a tree that is deeply tied to the maintaining and passing on of knowledge. In fact, the words *beech* and *book* have the same root. Its bark is very thin and easy to carve on; unfortunately for the trees, this has led to the practice of people carving their lovers' names or commemorating events on the beech trees' bark. A less-damaging practice was to carve a wish into a found beech twig and drive it into the ground—and into the underworld for the consideration of the fae. In the British Isles, there is an old custom of tying wishes to the branches of beech trees, for it is known as a wishing tree.

The druids sometimes gathered amongst the stately pillars of beech groves as an alternative to oak groves, calling beech the mother of the woods, consort to the king oak. Beechnuts are edible, and like the hazelnut were believed to imbue wisdom. The nuts are slightly bitter, but not as bitter as acorns. The beech also has underworld connections. Its roots are very visible and snakelike as they push down into the lower realms. It also holds on to its dead leaves throughout the winter, dropping them in the spring, shortly before the new leaves arrive. It was believed that beech trees could not be struck by lightning; they actually are struck as often as other trees, but their physical makeup has made them excellent conductors of electricity, harmlessly grounding the lightning, with no damage to the tree.

Field Guide

The European beech or common beech (*Fagus sylvatica*) is considered a native to southern England, but it may have actually been introduced from other areas by Stone Age humans, who used the nuts as food while traveling. It is found all over Europe, and other varieties of beech are found in North America and Asia. Beeches are large trees, growing to heights of 160 feet, with trunks as big as 10 feet in diameter, its lower branches sometimes drooping to the ground. They can live between 150 and 200 years. They are mostly found in forest environments—the beech can't handle pollution, so it's seldom found in cities. The bark of the beech is thin, gray, and very smooth; its leaves are alternate and simple, with straight, parallel veining and shallow teeth. The beech flowers shortly after the leaves come on in the spring, with small green male and female catkins that are wind-pollinated. Beech trees produce catkins and seeds biannually.

The seeds are called beechnuts and are triangularly shaped, two growing together in a spiny cupule that matures in autumn. In the fall, its leaves turn an orange-coppery color and remain on the tree until spring, turning brown over the winter. When they fall to the ground, the nuts are eaten by small mammals, birds, deer, and wild boar. People don't eat them as often today as in the past; we now know that they would be mildly toxic if eaten in large amounts, due to their high tannin content. The beech is often planted as an ornamental tree and is also used for firewood and for carpentry—but only for indoor projects, as it doesn't stand up well to weather. Beech woodchips are used to age American lager beer.

Chapter 3

Λ Passage Through the Grove
Ogham Tree Devotionals
and a Meditation

here are two devotionals and a meditation technique that you can use to enlist the energies of the trees of the ogham to surround you, lend you strength, and bless you with protection, guidance, and energy. The two devotionals are simple rituals that have been field-tested and found to be remarkably powerful tools; when you enlist the power of the trees with respect and honor, it is a force to be reckoned with. These can be used anytime that you wish, whether you feel vulnerable or you just need an extra boost of spirit. You can also use either of these as a daily or weekly devotional. What could be more natural than calling upon the trees of the earth to bolster and strengthen our spirits?

The Summoning of Trees is an adaptation of the classic Lesser Banishing Ritual of the Pentagram (LBRP) used in high magic. It's a communion with the Divine, an exercise in concentration, and a powerful protection ritual that banishes negative forces and seals your psychic shield.

This version draws upon elemental and tree energy that aligns with traditional angelic correspondences. Carefully crafted to correspond to the purpose of the original LBRP, this ritual is a version in line with tree energy and was created with the natural-world counterparts of the traditional angelic forces. The specific trees were chosen according to their elemental and energetic qualities. This ritual may be performed daily or as needed. The first section aligns your energies and connects you with your higher power, the second part calls upon the elements to banish any negativity, and the third part summons a powerful sacred grove of protection around you.

It is a quick yet powerful ritual that only takes a couple of minutes. You may place the corresponding cards at the cardinal points if you wish, but you don't have to. Many of the people I have shared it with wrote the words on a small business card–sized piece of paper that they could hold in their hand throughout the ritual until they had it memorized.

The Summoning of Trees

Stand facing east. Take a deep breath, feel your roots growing down from your feet into the ground, and feel branches extending upwards from your aura into the sky. When you point in this ritual, it is with your forefinger and second finger together, your thumb alongside your index finger; this is a sacred gesture. The pentagram used in this ritual is a symbol of the four elements—air, fire, water, and earth; the top point represents spirit above all.

Point up above your head, and say: "As above."

Point down to the ground: "So below."

Touch right shoulder: "To extend without."

Touch left shoulder: "To draw within."

Touch solar plexus: "The grove is my strength."

Cup your hands at your solar plexus: "I am one."

Still facing east, with first and second finger together, draw a yellow pentagram. Visualize a forest beyond it, leaves rustling in the breeze, and say: "Winds of the east."

Keep your arm extended, and rotate to the right.

Facing south, draw a red pentagram. Visualize a forest beyond it, sunshine coming through the leaves, and say: "Fire of the south."

Keep your arm extended, and rotate to the right.

Facing west, draw a blue pentagram. Visualize a forest beyond it at the edge of a bluff, the water crashing on the shore, and say: "Seas of the west."

Keep your arm extended, and rotate to the right.

Facing north, draw a green pentagram. Visualize a forest beyond it, with mountains towering above the treetops, and say: "Mountains of the north."

Keep your arm extended, and rotate to the right, completing the circle, and end up facing east again.

Arms outstretched, palms facing the sky, feet spread about a foot apart, repeat the following:

"Before me, the blessed alder.
Behind me, the sacred apple.
On my right hand, the ash of victory.
On my left hand, the mighty oak."

You are now the pillar of the world tree. Visualize a bright light shining at your solar plexus.

Announce: "About me stands the sacred grove. Upon the column stands the shining star of force and fire!"

Point up above your head: "As above."

Point down to the ground: "So below."

Touch right shoulder: "To extend without."

Touch left shoulder: "To draw within."

Touch solar plexus: "The grove is my strength."

Connect the fingertips of both hands together, fingers slightly spread and pointing down, before your solar plexus, and say: "I am one."

Take a deep, cleansing breath in and out.

Those who already perform the Lesser Banishing Ritual of the Pentagram (LBRP) will probably notice that the energy of this ritual is a little different and operates on a slightly different vibrational level. I've noticed that the LBRP feels stellar to me, while the Summoning of Trees feels very earthy and warm.

The Lorica of the Trees was also inspired by a traditional ritual. A lorica is a special kind of prayer that invokes specific powers for protection. *Lorica* is another name for breastplate, as in armor, and can be invoked to create a powerful shield against anything from psychic attack to office politics or petty gossip. During my research for this deck, I came across the Lorica of St. Patrick, which I found to be quite fascinating, because in this prayer the powers of the elements are invoked, and it actually is worded like a spell for protection. There is one theory, not yet proven, that parts of the wording may have been lifted from old Celtic folk magic protection rituals. It isn't beyond the realm of possibility, since Patrick lived in Pagan Ireland as a youth. Patrick's great understanding of the Celtic tribal culture and indigenous religions was actually what made him such an effective missionary. I liked the idea of possibly reclaiming some of that wisdom and applying it in a new lorica based on the tree ogham in honor of the old tribes and the land.

Like the Summoning of Trees, you may use this lorica anytime you wish. Its structural energy is much like a verbal version of walking a labyrinth. Once you enter it, it carries you on a spiritual journey within and brings you back out again where you first entered. The best way to perform this exercise is to simply recite it out loud; reading it directly is fine. You may put your cards in order and flip through them as each tree is mentioned if you wish.

The Lorica of the Trees

I arise today
Through a mighty strength, the
  invocation of the sacred grove
Through a belief in its power and
  the power of the universe
Through every aspect of the Divine and the Oneness
And of the Lord and Lady of the growing earth.

I arise today
Through the strength of the ancient stones
In obedience of the universal laws
In service to my higher power
In hope of enlightenment
In the legacy of the ancients
In the teachings of the elders
In faith and fellowship of the earth
In innocence of the laughter of children
In deeds of brave men and women.

I arise today
Through the strength of the heavens
Light of the sun
Splendor of fire
Speed of lightning

Swiftness of the wind
Depth of the sea
Stability of the earth
Firmness of the rock.

I arise today
Through the strength of Ogma's grove of wisdom:
Birch to renew me
Rowan to shield me and mine from all harm
Alder's wisdom to guide me
Willow's eyes to look before me
Ash to activate my will
Hawthorn to defend me
Oak's power to open the way for me
Holly to strengthen me in adversity
Hazel as my inspiration
Apple to give me sanctuary
Vine to nourish my body and soul
Ivy to remind me who I am
Broom and reed to bless my body and home
Blackthorn as a barrier from danger
Elder to make me aware of my actions
Silverfir and elm help me honor the wonders of life
Gorse to bolster my wild heart
Heather to guide me into faithful fellowship

Aspen to awaken my courage
Yew to protect my mortality
The entire grove to keep me balanced
Spindle to remind me of my obligations
Gooseberry to bless my success
Woodbine to reveal the secrets of my book of dreams
Beech to make of me both student and teacher.

I summon today all these powers between me
   and those who would harm me and mine
Against any cruel and merciless power
   that opposes my body and soul
Against angry plans of misguided people
Against the use of any power invoked out
   of fear or aggression or jealousy
Against my own misgivings and fears
   that may cause my own harm.

The grove with me
The grove before me
The grove behind me
The grove in me
The grove's roots beneath me
The grove's branches above me
The grove all around me.

Goodness in the heart of everyone who thinks of me
Goodness in the mouth of everyone who speaks of me
Goodness in the eye that sees me
Goodness in the ear that hears me.

I arise today
Through a mighty strength, the
    invocation of the sacred grove
Through a belief in its power and
    the power of the universe
Through every aspect of the Divine and the Oneness
And of the Lord and Lady of the growing earth.

Meditating with the Trees

You may find that there is a particular card or tree energy that you wish to explore more deeply. These images can be used as meditation tools to find a deeper mental connection to the tree you wish to work with. In working with the ogham, it can be of great benefit to explore the individual tree's spirits and lessons as well as look at the system as a grove of trees, each part making up the whole.

Before meditating upon an image, read this book's entry for the card you are working with to better acquaint yourself with the mythic tree energies of that card. Then, find a quiet place where you will not be disturbed—somewhere outside would be lovely, but it's not necessary. If you wish, light a candle and/or a stick of incense, whatever may help you relax. This exercise is an extension of the work you did when you dedicated your deck, journeying deeper into the mysteries of the tree and the ogham.

Place the card you wish to work with in front of you so that you can easily see it while sitting comfortably on the floor or ground. You will now ground and center yourself. Close your eyes and clear your mind; imagine that you can feel your spirit within your body. Begin to pull it in tight within you. Focus on your solar plexus, which is the point about halfway between the base of your sternum and your navel; this is your personal energy center. Allow your spirit to align with your solar plexus. Now gently release your spirit back out to its original expansion, feeling it aligning properly within your physical body as it goes. You are now centered.

Now, in order to ground, imagine that there are roots growing down from the place where your body meets the floor. Those roots, as they grow down deep, will begin to form a deep connection with the earth, much like a tree does. An exchange of energy will take place: all the negative and unhealthy energy you may be storing will flow down the roots and into the earth to be neutralized, and now you may draw up fresh earth energy. Feel it filling you until it flows up to the sky. Like a tree, you are now connected to the higher and lower realms, and you are grounded and ready for your tree meditation.

Now you may open your eyes and gaze upon the card, opening yourself to both the image before you and the tree energy it represents. Ask the spirit of the particular tree to teach you the lesson that it has to share with you as you study the image on the card. Explore every detail of the image carefully. Now, as you close your eyes, keep the image in your head as you watch more of the scene unfold. You may hear the wind rustling the leaves, you may smell the forest, the characters may have messages for you—your impressions may be very vivid or simply a feeling or thought. When you are ready, you may open your eyes and look at the card once again, confirming your return to the physical realm. Thank the spirit of the tree and turn the card over, indicating the end of the meditation.

Chapter 4

Ogham Cree Magic

These cards have all been infused with the magic of the trees they represent. You can use them not only for divination and meditation, but also to send positive transformation into the world by accessing the connections to the trees. There are several ways these cards can be used for magical transformation. Choosing the card you wish to use for magic depends on what kind of change you want to manifest. For instance, if you are looking for protection, the rowan card is perfect. Are you facing a fear? Try focusing on the aspen card. If you need healing and rest, maybe the apple card can help you choose just the right peaceful sanctuary.

You can prop up the card next to a candle. Lighting the candle, ask the tree spirit you are working with to bring the specific transformation you are asking for into your life. You can also place the card in a prominent place where you can see it and perform a daily devotion, enlisting the tree energy and your higher spirit to help you attain your goals. Another great way to use a card for a specific purpose would be to use it for dream magic. Study the card right before going to sleep and leave it near your bed, asking the tree spirit to show you the solution to your problem in a dream. Make sure you immediately write down anything you remember the next morning before you get out of bed.

Now I offer you a few simple examples of tree magic that can be done using the cards of this deck to affect positive change in your life. Feel free to come up with magic of your own using the cards. Try adding berries, leaves, or a small piece of wood from the tree you are working with if you have access to it or one of its close relatives listed in the field guides. The following spells will give you an idea of how to incorporate these ogham cards into your own magic.

Healing:
Apple and Broom/Reed Cards

Use either a white or apple-scented tealight candle. Carve the apple ogham onto the top of the candle along with the broom/reed ogham. Set the apple and broom/reed cards on either side of the candle. Light the tealight and, focusing your intent, recite the divining charms for the apple, then the broom/reed, to activate the tree energies. Focus on healing mind, body, and spirit, filling your body and home with shining light. Allow the candle to burn out.

Find the Answer to a Question:
Alder and Willow Cards

Before going to bed, place a pen and paper near your bed and fill a crystal glass with water. Set the alder card on the left and the willow card on the right, next to each other and next to your bed where you can easily see them. With your right hand, put your pinky finger on willow and your ring finger on ash, and say:

> *I invoke the power of alder and willow within*
> *Answer my question as my dreams begin.*

Dip your finger in the crystal glass and run it around the rim until the crystal begins to sing; when it does, state the question you want an answer to. When you're ready, drink the water and go to sleep. When you awaken, write down any impressions you have received from your dreams; your answer will be within them.

Protection Talisman:
Rowan Card

Place a clear, flat glass marble (available at craft stores; we used to call them dragon's tears) on a piece of red paper and trace the outline, then cut it out, trimming it a little bit smaller. Using a black waterproof marker, draw the rowan ogham in the middle of the marble-sized circle of red paper. Using a decoupage medium, stick it to the flat side of the marble with the ogham toward the glass so that when it dries, you can see the ogham under the glass dome. Decoupage the back of the paper as well, and allow it to dry.

Place the completed talisman next to the rowan card and a red tealight candle with the rowan ogham carved on top. Light the candle and repeat the divining charm for the rowan to activate the tree energy; then, at the end, recite:

> *Spirit of rowan, imbue this talisman true*
> *Shield me on my journeys through all that I do.*

Allow the candle to burn out, and carry the talisman in your pocket for protection and as a psychic shield from harm. Repeat the ritual if you want to add an extra charge.

Bringing Love:
Heather and Woodbine Cards

To open your heart to allow love to come to you, place a pink candle in between the heather and woodbine cards. Carve both symbols onto the candle, and place a vase of woodbine nearby if it is in bloom. Light the candle. First, recite the woodbine's divining charm to open your eyes to all the possibilities, then recite the heather charm to bring a loyal and mutually beneficial partner. At the end, say:

Bring me a love that is right for me
For the greatest good, so shall it be.

Do not name any names or focus on someone you have in mind. Allow the candle to burn down. Keep the woodbine in your home until the blooms wilt, then keep a small piece of the stem in your pocket. Keep your eyes and your heart open to love coming your way. It may come from where you least expect it.

Prosperity:
Gooseberry and Vine Cards

Place the vine and gooseberry cards on either side of a green tealight candle with the oghams for both carved on it. Using a black pen, draw both the vine and gooseberry oghams on two dollar bills and lay both cards next to each other, on top of the bills. Light the candle. First, recite the vine's divining charm to offer gratefulness for what you have. Second, recite the divining charm for the gooseberry card, and visualize yourself already having all the abundance that you need to support yourself, with a little extra to spare. Allow the candle to burn down. Take one of the dollars and donate it to the first charity box you find. Keep the second dollar in a side pocket of your wallet, and don't spend it; remember that there is plenty in the universe for all, and allow it to come to you.

Unlock Your Success:
Oak, Ash, and Hawthorn Cards

This magical triad of trees can unlock your potential to overcome obstacles in your path and achieve success in your endeavors. In addition to the cards, you'll need a yellow candle (beeswax is ideal) and an old key. Take a permanent fine-tip marker and carefully draw a line along the key's blade, adding the ogham marks for oak, ash, and thorn along the line. Lay out the cards and the key near the lit candle, and meditate on these three trees. Hawthorn teaches you to be wary of opposition and deal with it with wisdom. Ash teaches you to take action when necessary. Oak teaches you to embrace your strength and step through the door of success without fear; your key is the balance of the three. Let the candle burn down. The key is now a talisman for your success—carry it with you.

Healing the Earth:
The Grove Card

When we truly listen to the voice of the trees, not only the trees of the ogham but all the trees of this planet, we are listening to our own roots, reminding us of the concept of oneness connecting everything together. If we believe that humankind rules our domain, this planet, let us rethink this. The idea that the "king and the land are one" permeates mythology for a reason. If we destroy our domain, our own destruction is close behind. In addition to the physical action that we need to take to protect our domain—the trees, waters, and life of this planet—we can also send spiritual energy toward that goal of protecting this vast sacred grove that we call Earth.

Print a photograph of Earth taken from space. Prop it up next to the grove card so that they're both easily seen. Carve the koad/grove symbol on a light blue candle and place it in a holder before the images, and surround it with a few twigs, rocks, and leaves you have gathered. Focusing on the candle flame, visualize all of Earth connected and receiving protection and healing. Recite the divination charm of the grove card to activate the tree energy, focusing on your intent. Allow the candle to burn out.

Now you've sent the magic and said the words. You've studied the trees and the lessons they have to offer. But that's not the end of the magic, for magic follows the path of least resistance. As you make your way in the world, this grand sacred grove within which we all live, do what you can to keep it safe. We are the stewards of this planet. When we act in accord with intentions to protect our earth, we are doing the highest magic and truly heeding the voice of the trees. Bringing the mythos and energy of the ogham trees into your life makes them part of your journey. Through the generosity of their spirits, the voice of the trees will always speak to you.

Chapter 5

Card Layouts

A card layout is the pattern and order in which you place the cards for a reading. Arranging your cards in a layout can show you the patterns relating to your question; when we can see the pattern, we can answer the question. You will find that this twenty-five-card ogham system contains a full scope of issues to provide guidance in a reading. This means that you can get very powerful readings and that you may prefer to use smaller layouts. I designed these layouts for this deck using eight or fewer cards for this reason. Feel free to experiment if you have a large layout that you like to use, but bear in mind that you may be using half or more of the deck per reading.

When doing a reading for yourself or someone else, you may wish to acquire a small cloth to lay the cards out on, to protect them physically and spiritually. Begin by shuffling the cards thoroughly as you concentrate on the question or situation that you wish to gain insight into. You may offer to allow the client to cut the cards. Some readers prefer not to let others handle their cards, while other readers don't mind at all.

When using the following layouts, use the divinatory meanings provided in this book along with your intuition to interpret the meanings of the cards. Also pay attention to which position the cards occupy in the layout as described for each spread. For example, if you're looking for a job and the spindle card is in a position referring to your hopes and dreams, this is positive, but it's even more profound if it falls in a position indicating the outcome. Look for patterns to emerge that relate to your question, and notice possible connections between the cards. Often in a reading, you will find that the cards relate to each other in a way that gives you a fuller picture of the situation. Using the cards as a catalyst, sometimes you'll get a feeling that part of the meaning is more accurate for a particular reading; go with that. Allow the cards to speak to you.

Choose a question: Decide what you want to ask—a specific question, such as, "Will my finances improve?" or "Is love on my path?" You may wish to write it down and make notes on the reading to refer to later.

Choose a layout: This choice will depend on the complexity of your question and your personal preference.

Shuffle the deck: Make sure the cards are mixed well as you concentrate on your question; stop when your gut feeling tells you to.

Lay out the cards: Dealing off the top, put each card in its position of your chosen layout, face up unless otherwise stated in the layout. If you choose not to read reversals, turn the cards right-side up.

Read each card: Going through the cards in the order they were laid out, read each card, paying attention to the position they are in, the images and how they make you feel, and the divinatory meanings.

Observe connections: Once you've gone over each card individually, look at how they relate to each other. Look for patterns and connections, and decide how they tell the story of the energies around the question to determine the best course of action.

Now that you know how to use the cards in conjunction with the layouts, here are the layouts I've designed specifically for this deck.

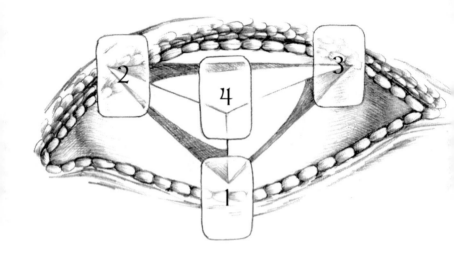

Dragon's Eye Spread

The dragon's eye is a symbol used to invoke dragon or fire-drake energy. The spirit of the dragon is associated with the earth in its entirety and represents the magnetic lines that run through the earth, known as ley lines, or dragon lines. The energy vortexes created by the convergences of these lines may have been sensed by the ancients, and they built their sacred sites upon them; Glastonbury Tor, Stonehenge, and even Sedona are located on ley lines. The Celts recognized three elements: earth, sky, and sea. Fire was a transformative entity, not actually an element.

The dragon's eye spread is a simple yet enlightening spread that can be used in a situation when you want to do a quick overview of a situation. It's a variation of the past, present, future spread.

1. The bottom point represents earth and the past source of the situation.

2. The left point represents sea and what is currently upon the shore.

3. The right point represents sky and how the situation will manifest in the future if the present course is maintained.

4. After you read the three cards, then lay the fourth in the middle, representing the dragon's fire of transformation, the powerful influence behind every aspect of the situation.

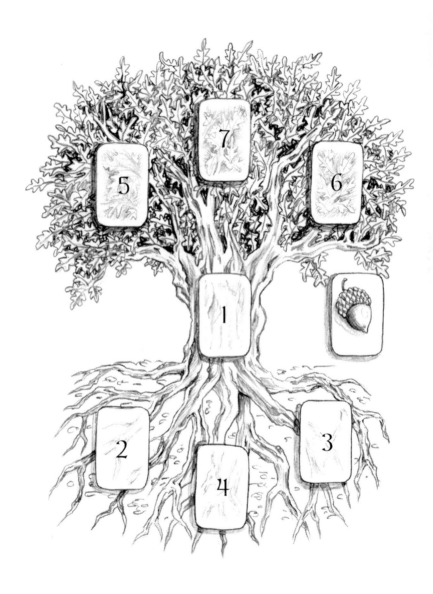

Oak Tree Spread

The oak tree has long been a sacred tree to the Celts. This layout helps you to see the deeper and higher aspects of a situation and offers an potential alternate outcome.

1. The trunk of the tree is the first position and represents the present situation.

2. The left roots are events of the past that led you here.

3. The right roots are unseen influences you may not have been aware of.

4. The middle roots are your deepest hopes or fears.

5. The left branches are a source of inspiration for the future.

6. The right branches are strength to draw upon—your best course of action.

7. The middle branches are the outcome if the current path is followed.

8. The acorn, representing the potential alternative outcome, is the outcome if the present course is changed.

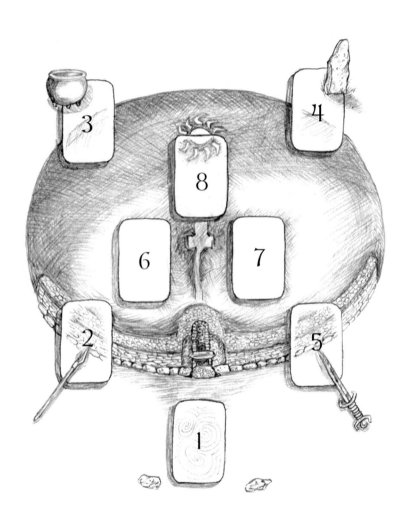

The Newgrange Spread

This divination spread is designed around the megalithic passage tomb for which it's named. Newgrange was estimated to have been built around 3200 BCE, according to carbon-14 dating from finds at the site. Amazingly, the ancients who built it aligned the passage leading to the center of the tomb with a purpose: when the sun rises on the winter solstice, a beam of light travels down the passage and illuminates the inner chamber—a stunning spectacle. This spread brings you on your quest to find your best course of action through exploring the cards that fall in the cardinal positions of the four treasures of the Tuatha de Danann. We then travel into the passage itself, to the three recesses of the chamber, discovering the outcome of the situation and a choice of the two different courses of action to apply to the outcome.

1. The Entrance Stone position represents yourself at the gateway of the situation and what brought you to the gate.

2. The Spear of Victory position in the south represents how others may be influencing the situation.

3. The Cauldron of Abundance position in the west represents financial influences and considerations as they relate to the situation.

4. The Stone of Destiny position in the north represents the hopes or fears that are your current focus.

5. The Sword of Truth position in the east represents what is unseen and the decision needed to overcome obstacles in your path.

6. The Left Recess position represents what may be gained if the outcome is guided by influences of emotional decisions.

7. The Right Recess position represents what may be gained if the outcome is guided by influences of intellectual decisions.

8. The end of the chamber finds us at the Central Recess of Newgrange, where a shaft of sunlight shines on the probable outcome of the situation.

Bibliography

Blamires, Steve. *Celtic Tree Mysteries: Practical Druid Magic & Divination.* St. Paul, MN: Llewellyn, 1997.

Bonwick, James. *Irish Druids and Old Irish Religions.* New York: Dorset, 1986.

Bulfinch, Thomas. *Bulfinch's Mythology, The Age of Fable, The Age of Chivalry, Legends of Charlemagne.* New York: Grosset & Dunlap, 1913.

Burne, Charlotte S. *The Handbook of Folklore.* London: Sidgwick & Jackson, 1914.

Cahill, Thomas. *How the Irish Saved Civilization: The Untold Story of Ireland's Heroic Role from the Fall of Rome to the Rise of Medieval Europe.* New York: Anchor Books/ Doubleday, 1996.

Conway, D. J. *By Oak, Ash, & Thorn: Modern Celtic Shamanism.* St. Paul, MN: Llewellyn, 1995.

———. *Celtic Magic.* St. Paul, MN: Llewellyn, 1990.

Cottrell, Leonard. *Roman Invasion of Britain.* New York: Dorset House, 1994.

Douglas, Ronald Macdonald. *The Scots Book.* New York: Senate Books, 1995.

Dugan, Ellen. *Garden Witch's Herbal: Green Magick, Herbalism & Spirituality.* Woodbury, MN: Llewellyn, 2009.

Frazer, Sir James George. *Illustrated Golden Bough: A Study in Magic and Religion.* New York: Simon & Schuster, 1996.

Gantz, Jeffrey, trans. *The Mabinogion.* New York: Dorset, 1985.

Geoffrey of Monmouth. *Vita Merlini: The Life of Merlin.* Trans. Basil Clarke. Cardiff: University of Wales, 1973.

Graves, Robert. *The White Goddess: A Historical Grammar of Poetic Myth.* New York: Farrar, Straus, and Giroux, 1948.

Greenaway, Kate. *Kate Greenaway's Language of Flowers.* New York: Merrimack, 2009.

Greer, John Michael. *The Druidry Handbook.* San Francisco: Red Wheel/Weiser, 2006.

Grieve, M. *A Modern Herbal: The Medicinal, Culinary, Cosmetic and Economic Properties, Cultivation and Folk-Lore of Herbs, Grasses, Fungi, Shrubs & Trees, With All Their Modern Scientific Uses.* New York: Dover Publications, 1971.

Hone, William. *Ancient Mysteries Described*. New York: Cosimo Classics, 2007.

Humphries, C. J. *Guide to Trees of Britain and Europe*. London: Hamlyn, 2000.

Kynes, Sandra. *Whispers from the Woods: The Lore and Magic of Trees*. Woodbury, MN: Llewellyn, 2006.

Lopez, Robert S. *The Birth of Europe*. New York: M. Evans and Company, 1966.

MacManus, Seumas. *The Story of the Irish Race: A Popular History of Ireland*. New York: The Devin-Adair Company, 1944.

Markale, Jean. *Celts: Uncovering the Mythic and Historic Origins of Western Culture*. Rochester, VT: Inner Traditions, 1993.

———. *Druids: Celtic Priests of Nature*. Rochester, VT: Inner Traditions, 1999.

Matthews, Caitlin, and John Matthews. *The Encyclopaedia of Celtic Wisdom: A Celtic Shaman's Sourcebook*. New York: Element Books, 1994.

Monroe, Douglas. *21 Lessons of Merlyn: A Study in Druid Magic & Lore*. St. Paul, MN: Llewellyn, 1992.

Mountfort, Paul Rhys. *Ogam, the Celtic Oracle of the Trees: Understanding, Casting, and Interpreting the Ancient Druidic Alphabet*. Rochester, VT: Destiny Books, 2002.

Mueller, Mickie. "Celtic Tree Lore." *Llewellyn's 2010 Witches' Datebook*. Woodbury, MN: Llewellyn, 2009.

―――. "A Little Bird Told Me: The Art of Ornithomany." *Llewellyn's 2011 Magical Almanac.* Woodbury, MN: Llewellyn, 2010.

Murray, Colin. *Celtic Tree Oracle: A System of Divination.* New York: St. Martin's, 1988.

Pennick, Nigel. *Celtic Sacred Landscapes.* London: Thames & Hudson, 1996.

Ross, Anne, and Don Robins. *Life and Death of a Druid Prince: The Story of Lindow Man, an Archaeological Sensation.* New York: Simon & Schuster, 1991.

Scherman, Katharine. *The Flowering of Ireland: Saints, Scholars, and Kings.* New York: Barnes & Noble, 1996.

Spence, Lewis. *Druids: Their Origins and History.* New York: Barnes & Noble, 1995.

Stewart, R. J. *Celtic Gods, Celtic Goddesses.* London: Blandford, 1990.

Streep, Peg. *Spiritual Gardening: Creating Sacred Space Outdoors.* Chicago: New World Library, 2003.

Tekiela, Stan. *Trees of Missouri Field Guide.* Cambridge, MN: Adventure Publications, 2006.

Thorsson, Edred. *Book of Ogham: The Celtic Tree Oracle.* St. Paul, MN: Llewellyn, 1992.

Website

www.treesforlife.org.uk. Trees for Life is an award-winning
charity working to help restore the Caledonian Forest,
which formerly covered a large part of the Scottish
Highlands. Just one percent of the original forest survives
today, as isolated stands of mostly old trees. Since 1989,
this organization has been helping to bring this forest
back from the brink, both through natural regeneration
and by planting trees. Their long-term vision is to restore
the forest, and all its constituent species, to a six-hundred-
square-mile area west of Inverness, including their ten-
thousand-acre Dundreggan Estate.

GET MORE AT LLEWELLYN.COM

Visit us online to browse hundreds of our books and decks, plus
sign up to receive our e-newsletters and exclusive online offers.

- **Free tarot readings • Spell-a-Day • Moon phases**
- **Recipes, spells, and tips • Blogs • Encyclopedia**
- **Author interviews, articles, and upcoming events**

GET SOCIAL WITH LLEWELLYN

Follow us on

Find us on
Facebook

twitter

www.Facebook.com/LlewellynBooks   www.Twitter.com/Llewellynbooks

GET BOOKS AT LLEWELLYN

LLEWELLYN ORDERING INFORMATION

Order online: Visit our website at www.llewellyn.com to select your books
and place an order on our secure server.

Order by phone:
- Call toll free within the U.S. at 1-877-NEW-WRLD (1-877-639-9753)
- Call toll free within Canada at 1-866-NEW-WRLD (1-866-639-9753)
- We accept VISA, MasterCard, and American Express

Order by mail:
Send the full price of your order (MN residents add 6.875% sales tax) in U.S. funds,
plus postage and handling to: Llewellyn Worldwide, 2143 Wooddale Drive
Woodbury, MN 55125-2989

POSTAGE AND HANDLING

STANDARD (U.S. & Canada):
(Please allow 12 business days)
$25.00 and under, add $4.00.
$25.01 and over, FREE SHIPPING.

INTERNATIONAL ORDERS (airmail only):
$16.00 for one book, plus $3.00 for
each additional book.

Visit us online for more shipping options.
Prices subject to change.

FREE CATALOG!

To order, call
1-877-
NEW-WRLD
ext. 8236
or visit our
website

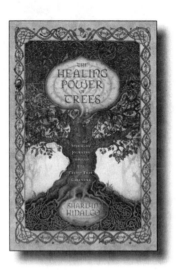

The Healing Power of Trees:
Spiritual Journeys Through the Celtic Tree Calendar

Sharlyn Hidalgo

Walk in the footsteps of Druids and tune in to the sacred power and ancient wisdom of trees.

From the birch to the willow, Sharlyn Hidalgo introduces all fifteen revered trees of the Celtic Tree Calendar and describes their unique gifts. Go on guided journeys to meet the deities, totems, and guides of each species. Honor each tree with rituals using runes and oghams, symbols and letters of the Celtic Tree Alphabet. Learn from the author's personal stories of revelation. Cultivate a relationship with each of these grand energetic beings, who offer healing, guidance, and higher consciousness.

The Healing Power of Trees is your guide to living the principles of the Celtic tradition—tuning in to the rhythms of nature, respecting the land, and fulfilling our role as stewards of our Earth.

978-0-7387-1998-6

$17.95, 6 x 9, 288 pp., illus., appendices, bibliog.

Flower and Tree Magic

Discover the Natural Enchantment Around You

Richard Webster

Flower and Tree Magic:
Discover the Natural Enchantment Around You

Richard Webster

Did you know that flowers have a unique language of their own? Or that the way you draw a tree reflects your life outlook and personality?

Flowers and trees have long been celebrated as sacred and powerful. By learning to read the special messages they hold, plants can help us navigate our life path and reconnect with nature. In this comprehensive guide, bestselling author Richard Webster uncovers the hidden properties of every major type of tree, herb, and flower that we encounter in our daily lives. From protection and healing to divination and worship, this book shows you how to apply ancient spiritual practices from many cultures to modern life—attract your ideal mate with valerian and sage, ward off psychic attacks with a sprinkling of rose oil, restore positive energy with nature meditations, and more.

Nature lovers, myth historians, and trivia lovers alike will embrace this all-encompassing guide to the vast history and extensive magic of flowers and trees.

978-0-7387-1349-6

$15.95, 6 x 9, 240 pp., index, bibliog.

To order, call 1-877-NEW-WRLD
Prices subject to change without notice
ORDER AT LLEWELLYN.COM 24 HOURS A DAY, 7 DAYS A WEEK!

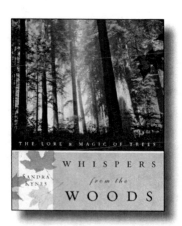

THE LORE & MAGIC OF TREES

WHISPERS
from the
WOODS

SANDRA
KYNES

Whispers from the Woods:
The Lore & Magic of Trees

Sandra Kynes

A walk in the woods makes it easy to understand the awe and reverence our ancestors had for trees. It speaks to something deep and primal within us—something we don't hear as often as we should.

By exploring a variety of mysteries and traditions of trees, *Whispers from the Woods* helps readers get reacquainted with the natural world and find their place in the earth's rhythm. Covering more than just Celtic Ogham and tree calendars, this book includes meditation, shamanic journeys, feng shui, spellcraft, and ritual. In addition, it has a reference section with detailed information on fifty trees, which includes seasonal information, lore, powers, attributes, and more.

978-0-7387-0781-5

288 pp., 7½ x 9⅛, $17.95

To order, call 1-877-NEW-WRLD
Prices subject to change without notice
ORDER AT LLEWELLYN.COM 24 HOURS A DAY, 7 DAYS A WEEK!

To Write to the Author

If you wish to contact the author or would like more information about this book, please write to the author in care of Llewellyn Worldwide, and we will forward your request. Both the author and the publisher appreciate hearing from you and learning of your enjoyment of this book and how it has helped you. Llewellyn Worldwide cannot guarantee that every letter written to the author can be answered, but all will be forwarded. Please write to:

Mickie Mueller
℅ Llewellyn Worldwide
2143 Wooddale Drive
Woodbury, MN 55125-2989
Please enclose a self-addressed stamped envelope for reply, or $1.00 to cover costs. If outside U.S.A., enclose international postal reply coupon.

Many of Llewellyn's authors have websites with additional information and resources. For more information, please visit our website:

HTTP://WWW.LLEWELLYN.COM

CPSIA information can be obtained at www.ICGtesting.com
Printed in the USA
BVOW04s2119250914

368033BV00003B/3/P